MY PHILOSOPHY OF MUSIC

HANNA KULENTY

≈ MY PHILOSOPHY OF MUSIC ≈

HANNA KULENTY

edited by
Maja Trochimczyk

Moonrise Press, 2024

Copyright Information

My Philosophy of Music by Hanna Kulenty is a collection of essays by the composer, edited and translated by Maja Trochimczyk and published by Moonrise Press.

P.O. Box 4288, Los Angeles – Sunland, CA 91041-4288, www.moonrisepress.com.

© Copyright 2024 by Hanna Kulenty and Maja Trochimczyk

All Rights Reserved 2024 by Moonrise Press for this collection only.

Cover design by Maja Trochimczyk, based on Hanna Kulenty's painting, *Muzyka grawitacyjna Nr 1*, acrylic on canvas, 2023. Font: Brittanic Bold on the cover and Cambria in the text.

No part of this book may be reproduced or utilized in any form or by any means, electronic or mechanical, including photocopying and recording, or by any information storage and retrieval system, without permission in writing from the author and publisher.

Manufactured in the United States of America

The Library of Congress Publication Data:

Hanna Kulenty (b. 1961), author / Maja Trochimczyk (b. 1957) editor and translator [in English.]
My Philosophy of Music. / Hanna Kulenty, author / Maja Trochimczyk, editor and translator

120 pages (vi pp. prefatory matter, and 114 pp.); 6in x 9in. Written in English. With a biography, list of works, discography and bibliography.

ISBN 978-1-945938-74-0 (paperback)
ISBN 978-1-945938-75-7 (hardcover)
ISBN 978-1-945938-76-4 (eBook)

10 9 8 7 6 5 4 3 2 1

≈ TABLE OF CONTENTS ≈

1. About the Polyphony of Arcs ≈ 3
2. On the Multidimensional Theory of Time (2003) ≈ 6
3. My Philosophy of Music (2015) ≈ 22
4. Between Kitsch and Surrealism (2017) ≈ 64
5. Maja Trochimczyk: Dimensions of Time and Emotion – The Music of Hanna Kulenty ≈ 75
6. A Biography of Hanna Kulenty ≈ 89
7. List of Works ≈ 99
8. Film and TV Music ≈ 106
9. Awards ≈ 107
10. Discography ≈ 109
11. Bibliography ≈ 111

≈ MY PHILOSOPHY OF MUSIC ≈

≈ ABOUT THE POLYPHONY OF ARCS ≈
Hanna Kulenty

First published in Kulenty's compositional brochures by PWM Edition, 1998, and Donemus, 2003

Polyphony of arcs. When I say 'arc,' I have some sort of emotional structure in mind. An arc design would be a way of expressing the intensity curve or energy of a particular structure. A single work could, of course, be built from such a structure, but I am interested in the combination and overlapping of such structures.

An arc is simply a structure of a defined emotional course, of a defined climate, containing a climax. At the same time, an arc does not have to follow a classical course — from the introductory phrase, through the climax up to the last sounds. It may begin at any place, for example from the climax. Certainly, however, the duration of the sound depends on the density of events in the climax. I like to write very much as if the work began from the middle, from the climax. Only later does everything fall into an order in which every arc has its own length, develops in its own way and by no means simultaneously. This is exactly how both of my symphonies are constructed.

I use my own harmony, which means I use certain chords, and in this case the type of arc is determined by the tempo in which these chords appear. Let's take *Sesto* for piano: there certain chords change very slowly, forming one arc. The tempo in which other chords change is considerably faster — therefore a second arc is formed. And so on. Simply, because of the different tempos of chord sequences various types of emotions are evoked. The same will happen if, for example, we bring in various rhythms — they also determine the quality of energy, therefore they permit the construction of a defined structure. In percussion works, the arcs are sonorous, — I combine the various colors, for example, wooden, metallic, membrane... But of course, I use different types of arcs in every work.

A polyphony of arcs is an overlapping of several arcs, combined in such a way that the work as a whole will have the from of an arc. I also try to arrange the climaxes of particular arcs in succession one after another, so that something like a permanent climax is formed. That permanent climax, of course, has its own energy course, and it develops in a defined way. Besides, the concept of climax can be understood in different ways. In the classical meaning, it links with plurality, a collection of something. At the same time, for example in *Quatro*, the climax of an arc depends on the fact that other events disengage themselves or are brought together to a rhythmical unison. So, the climax here is a cleansing of perception. In the fourth arc (the work is composed of four arcs, thus the title *Quatro*) a general pause appears at the point of climax. In this case, therefore, the climax is silence.

I was consciously exploring these techniques in *Sesto* right after the performance of *Ad unum*. It was extremely important that I could hear my music, and because of this I wrote *Sesto, Quatro, Quinto, Arci.* However, later those arcs of mine got into my blood, and I stopped thinking about them. I simply sit down and write. Actually, already *Ad unum* was created from the beginning to the end without anything crossed out. The only change was that I rewrote the pencil version in ink. Today I write right away in ink. I am sure of what I do, of what I hear. Just in case, though, I begin writing a work by notating all arcs on a card. I simply write about the whole work in words. But once a work exists, I don't change it. I never change music, although it does happen that I apply simpler ways of performing it or a simpler notation.

I once analyzed the material within an arc and it appeared that the same controlling basis operates throughout. Arcs are stronger than I am, it's something that is in my subconsciousness. I have it somehow coded. I really didn't invent this. Simply a breath and expiration — to inhale and to exhale — the natural pulse or rhythm of a human being. I feel everything in this way. I even arrange chords in order to form a relation of breath and expiration. In general, I first hear sounds and colors, then when I try Lo remember these, I see these arcs. I actually do "hear" the musical work in its entirely. Everything all once. As if time didn't exist at all...

Naturally, I can later listen to the work in my mind as if from a tape — from the beginning to the end, in real time. Some believe that I invent arcs from the start, and later I think about how to fill them in. But that's not true.

~ Hanna Kulenty

≋ ON THE MULTI-DIMENSIONAL ≋
≋ THEORY OF TIME ≋

Hanna Kulenty in Coversation with Maja Trochimczyk

August 2003, Arnhem, the Netherlands, transcribed and translated by Maja Trochimczyk

Maja Trochimczyk: *We are in the beautiful summer garden of a house in Arnhem, full of interplay of sunlight and shadows among the trees. We arrived here from different places — I came from Los Angeles, you were recently in Warsaw. We have known each other since our first year of studies at the Fryderyk Chopin Academy of Music. Quite a long time. So, let's talk about time. I know that the "polyphony of time" is one of the most important foundations of your compositional technique. Can you explain?*

Hanna Kulenty: I came up with a theory of six basic categories or types of time. Let me tell you about them one by one. The first "type of time" is the sound spectrum: that is the time of pedal notes in the piano, or in the orchestra. This time is, as it were, at a standstill. There is just the presence of sound, no obvious motion. Then, there arises a possibility that these low sounds will be amplified from time to time by other instruments, which means that we can expect that the harmonic components of the fundamental tone would appear somewhere else in the orchestra. Then, with the gradual appearance and disappearance of these added harmonics in different colors the time would begin to slowly evolve while still being somewhat static. But even if you hear such a pedal note alone, without the support of other instruments highlighting its different harmonics, you can say that it is the basic type of time of "being present," in a very elongated form.

The second "type of time" consists of binary rhythms — ta-ta ta-ta — ta-ta... This temporal layer can also be divided into additional elements. In the score, I may write a flat with an arrow and a flat with a cross, and this is how I would write down this double time stratification. Here, in the repeated rhythm of these "doubles," a new, different, temporal layer appears.

The third dimension or type of time is triple time created by the triplet rhythm, when notes are repeated in triplets, with accents, crescendos and changes in pitch: ta-ta-ta — ta-ta-ta — ta-ta-ta. These triple rhythms can be mixed with double time of paired notes in twos. I can mix the "double" and "triple" dimensions of time — if we were to describe it in a cube of temporal dimensions, we would be moving from one edge of the cube to the other, from one temporal-rhythmic dimension to the next. Here, time begins to shift and can be moved back either gradually or suddenly. In the latter case, the temporal shift of rhythmic patterns may create the effect of a certain "jump" — and the impression of surprise for the listener.

The next type of time is the division of the temporal flow into four elements, which I write down using an appropriately transformed notation system — with cancel signs, sharps and flats. It may be called the quadruple time. While listening to these transitions from one dimension of time to another, we are able to feel that at a certain moment the musical material belongs to one layer — for example, a layer of triplets, and at the next moment a binary material appears. These differences in temporal dimensions feel very clear in the audible flow of the music. Temporal layers shift suddenly, from one "type of time" to another, in something that resembles a seismic "leap" — and this is how a specific style of music is created.

If we compare these temporal layers with the element of pitch, this juxtaposition of different types of time is equivalent to a juxtaposition of a "white cluster" in one layer with a "black cluster" in another layer. Here, the "white" and "black" refer to the notes on the piano keyboard, of curse. So, the "white" scale would begin on C and the "black" on C-sharp. Their co-presence is easy to feel; these elements belong to different harmonic dimensions, or — in the case of "types of time" — to different temporal dimensions. After measuring time in fourths (or quadruples) in the multidimensional space of time, there follow divisions into fives (quintuple time) and sixes (sextuple time). Then, in the next temporal layer, the rhythm may be again divided into smaller values, and we may fill this gradually fragmented flow of time with ever diminishing units. We may thicken it or make it thinner, thus descending or ascending between various "types of time" on unique "temporal stairs" — the dimensions of rhythmic units, that may be divided down to the last, shortest unit of sound.

Temporal shifts "beyond" the gradual fragmentation and condensation of temporal units, for example leaping from sixths to fourths or twos, make a huge impression on the listeners. The leaps from one type of time to another then become sudden, clearly noticeable, musical events. The effect is as if the listeners had fallen off something, as if they were surprised by an unexpected change. Let's imagine that you are flying in a plane and the plane suddenly falls into an air hole, rapidly dropping its altitude. Depending on the size of the air hole and the depth of the fall, the effect of surprise for the passengers (or listeners, in the case of music) would be stronger or weaker. Sometimes it would be huge — when the change in the plane's elevation (or, in the case of my music, in the distance separating the types of time) is large enough. Then, we would have enormous leaps, up and down these "temporal stairs." In other cases, these changes occur gradually, step by step, so we could have tiny steps. It all depends on the distance between the starting point and the destination point; the initial and the final stratum of time.

MT: *That's very interesting. Do you have any specific musical examples of how it works in practice?*

HK: I applied these theories of multidimensional layers of time for the first time in the Trumpet Concerto. When composing this piece, I had a vision of its overall form and flowe in time, and then I made a preliminary plan and calculated these temporal layers. I counted exactly what types of time and tempos would appear in the piece, how many measures were needed for the whole concerto and how many for individual sections. I write my music in full measures, so I had to calculate it exactly: when divided into 4 units and with a tempo of 144, there were at least 36 bars. As you see, first, before I fill the music score with specific notes, I envision and write down the overall time structure — I need to know how time will flow during the piece, from what dimension I will go to the next...

MT: *So, when composing, you first plan the entire piece "from a bird's eye view," right? I remember you once told me that when you create a new piece, initially it appears as a complete whole in your "mind's eye" — your imagination. It has a form, like a spatial-temporal sound sculpture, and you have to write it down very quickly, in a hurry, in order to describe that overall shape exactly with notes...*

HK: Yes, I remember that. And then you cited Rilke's "An die Musik" — which talks about music as a sound sculpture. How do you construct such a spatio-temporal shape? In music, composition deals with time: you need to know what is supposed to happen, where and when, at what moment, in what second. However, this cannot be done in the form of an abstract structure, which is only later filled with material... That interpretation is incorrect. The material is music from the beginning, but it needs to be formed, limited and arranged in time. In music, time is of the essence; that's why I write down, calculate and plan how much time will appear in the new piece, what the proportions would be, where the climax of the greatest tension would be located, etc. First I plan, and then I know where I am. However, I do many things automatically, since I have intuition about musical form and the planning of musical time. For example, the "golden section" point two-thirds of the way through the work — I do not have to plan it or calculate it, I do not have to worry about it. The music flows almost automatically to this climactic moment; composing in such classical proportions is like flying on an "autopilot" for me.

Thanks to the shifts and changes of the "types of time", the whole piece takes on its form and the music gains its shape. For example, at some point in the music, I suggest a certain spectrum, a continuous sound. We listen to its interior, seeking out its internal, harmonic elements. At the beginning, I reveal all the components of the spectrum, but in subsequent "reincarnations" of this spectrum, only the appearance of its basic tone, the lowest note, may be enough to remind the listeners of its entire dimensions, the entire static layer of time. Its harmonic components no longer need to be consciously analyzed and presented in their entirety. The allusions to the initial spectrum already suggest a certain direction, the presence of certain elements.

MT: *Here, you're talking about allusions, reminders, that is, about the listeners' anticipation or expectation of musical elements that may suddenly appear and disappear. Actually, this reminds me of a theory proposed in 1956 by Leonard B. Meyer, his theory of musical expectancy, in which musical meaning arises from the music's capacity to generate, suspend, prolongate, or violate the listeners' expectations. Can we say that, when composing a new piece, you immediately think* *about what it would sound like and what its effect would be on your listeners? Am I correct?*

HK: Of course! The effect of such allusions and play with the listeners' expectations depends on whether a given element is predictable or not. In a sense, it must be predictable, which means that the listener, having learned the characteristics of a certain temporal layer, will later expect that same layer to recur in the piece. The listener is carried away by this repeated rhythm, this particular type of time. It becomes as natural as the breathing process; the listener enters into a trance. The continuity and repetition of rhythms in the "spectral", "double" or "triple" temporal layers become the basic dimensions of the musical work, ensuring its identity and existence. However, sudden changes between these temporal layers, unexpected jumps from one temporal dimension, one "type of time" to another, may cause a surprise and break off this trance. This is essential in the perception of music.

Let us return to my analogy of an airplane flight. The air holes that the plane falls into shock the passengers, startle them from their naps, from reading. The drop in altitude draws their attention to their state of being in flight above the ground, to their actual absurd situation — they are inside a huge, metal machine high above the surface of the Earth. Similarly, such sudden shifts from one temporal dimension to another cause a "refreshing" or a renewal of perception, a renewed focus on the sound itself, musical reality and its actual form. As I said, the further these temporal layers are from each other, the stronger the effect.

I must add here that such deepening of the shift-and-shock effect works only within certain limits. The temporal layers that are connected by these shifts must have common elements that they share. They must be quite close to each other. The "types of time" must be homogeneous to some extent and cannot be too far apart. Without such common elements, in the condition of a total distance and enormous contrast, there would be no sense of a connection between one temporal layer and another. It is their elementary commonality at a given level — that is not obvious, not clearly noticeable "on the surface" of the music — that creates the sense of surprise.

The listeners do not expect to hear a completely new material and when they notice a certain change, they may begin to wonder and think: "Why exactly? Where did this completely new material come from? What does that even mean?" This moment of the listeners' involvement in the active analysis of their impressions created by musical elements that they had listened to with a certain passivity, causes them to enter deeper into the reality of the musical piece, into the interior of the language and structure of music. Thus, these sudden shifts causing the listeners to awaken to the perception of the "essence of things" are beyond the limits of their awareness and expectations. The shifts of temporal layers are completely unpredictable, disturbing the listeners from their natural attitude of expectation, directed towards the continuity of rhythm, texture, or the entire piece.

MT: *Fascinating. The music you compose, even though you talk about abstract theories of time dimensions, is actually very focused on its listeners, on your audience. You write for someone who listens. You look for a way for your concept of music to reach them through sound...*

HK: Yes, after all, music is not for viewing at an exhibition. It exists in the sounds that someone plays and someone else listens to. Coming back to my compositional technique, I like these effects of shifting layers of time and I know how to compose them. In my music, I often introduce a new layer, which is seemingly distant and different, but the listeners feel that they have already encountered this material somewhere before. It is always a game in the subconscious. I write my music while realizing that it must constantly work with the listeners' awareness, that there must be hidden elements in the musical composition that unite it into an organic, multidimensional whole.

I think that we sometimes don't use time at all in our awareness. A person like that does not live, they just vegetate... In these situations, you just exist and you don't wonder why, where... Time only determines what you have to do at a certain moment — you don't even think that you are a slave of time. I think about the past and I am in the past. I remember it I relive it. I'm flooded with memories, with the past, and therefore I cannot grasp the present. I'm supposed to be happy about something, but I can't because I'm burdened by the past dimension of time. I think about the past and remember what happened, or I think about the future. I am happy about something or afraid of something. I am never in the present, in my own time, in that time in which I actually exist and breathe. In this way, the present ceases to exist and disappears from consciousness. You see, it depends on what we focus our attention on, where we look. My music allows the listeners to "shift" their perspective, to become aware of the reality of existence, the reality of time. Thanks to the multidimensionality of temporal layers, we are able to focus on the point of "now"— where all times converge into the infinity point, the zero point.

MT: *"All times converge..." this statement reminds me of Giordano Bruno and his reflections on the infinity of the Universe, the co-existence of the point, the center and the sphere surrounding the point, with its circumference. They are dynamically related, as the point expands into the circumference and the sphere collapses into the point. Interesting. Then, "zero point" in military terms means "he location of the center of a burst of a nuclear weapon at the* *instant of detonation." In cosmology, it is the point from which Bing Bang commences, as everything comes into being from the one point, or nothing... The implications of your theory are quite far-reaching.*

HK: No, do not go so far. I'd like to be less speculative and stick to human perception of the world and in particular, to the perception of music. Let me explain it again, using a different analogy. When you're riding a train and you look out the window, you may focus on the trees close to the windows. Then, you just see a blur. The train goes too fast. You cannot differentiate or remember exactly what's flashing before your eyes at a great speed. Neither can you think about what's going to happen. You are unable to track changes and have no sense of what is happening. But if you look further away, towards the horizon, you perceive what is visible from a broader perspective of another dimension, greater distance. In this case, you not only see the whole distant forest on the horizon, but you also see what is quickly moving in the near plane. You are able to perceive all the changes taking place in this "foreground" layer.

It is as if you were looking at the entire space at the same time, in all its dimensions — what is close by, and what is far away. So, you can say: "I look ahead at myself, or, I see, I move, or I move further..." There is a clear focus there. But you also see me at the same time — initially I am, to you, only a blurred image, and this doesn't matter, but then you can focus on the background and through that focus you can perceive what is in the foreground, as well. And, thanks to focusing on the overall image, looking far away at the horizon, you have time and ability to observe also what constantly shifts close by. You can notice what's going on here, one element after another, one by one. It's annoying, but it's just the way it is.

When you look into the distance, you see something completely different from what appears and shifts in the foreground. Only then you can see it better. It is because you do not try so hard. You do not force yourself: "I have to see it... I have to feel it..." No. And that's it. When the effort is too great and you have to strain our eyes, your vision becomes much worse and you lose the ability to see.

I relate this to my music: its course is perceived similarly at close proximity and from afar, as if looking into the distance and into the foreground at the same time (with "extended" and "drawn in" eyesight). You may see everything simultaneously, both far and near. You see the foreground elements, you notice them, although you focus on the main line visible (or audible) in the distance. This is the overall dimension of the whole composition. The interplay and change of these "layers" or "types" of time introduces the multiplicity of temporal dimensions: simultaneity, three-dimensionality, and multi-dimensionality of time.

This is where the real temporal multidimensionality comes into play — here, a different way of perceiving time emerges. First, there is a line, then there is a square, then there is a cube. There is a time that is inside another type or dimension of time: time in a square, time in a cube, and so on. In the accumulating temporal dimensions, these layers of time overlap and accumulate more and more, until they create a full temporal sphere. This "sphere" of time dimensions can rotate forward and backward, shifting to the future or to the past. Then, individual dimensions of time are like lines with a common beginning, which are at first closer to each other, but then move away and become more and more distant from each other.

MT: *This theory is quite complicated. All possible times, all possible temporal dimensions coexisting in one sphere of time that can be perceived as moving forward or backward... As T.S.*

Eliot wrote in the Four Quartets: *""Time present and time past / Are both perhaps present in time future / And time future contained in time past." Is this what you mean? Or do you have another way of describing these layers or dimensions of time?*

HK: So you want to show off your erudition? OK, there is something to it... Let's try again, Imagine these multiple timelines while looking at your watch. Inside, there are pointers on the axis. On the plane around the axis, there are numbers, but you can also look vertically up or down from this plane. Now, you may add two extra lines to your flat plane. There is a circle with its center and the vertical lines intersect with the circle in its central point, the axis. And now, if the lines with a common center move away from this plane of the circle more and more, and shift to a different angle, the distance between them will also gradually become larger. Next, imagine that this vertical line is not just a line, but it is placed on the surface of the second, vertical circle, penetrating the first, horizontal circle at a right angle. Now, you will also be able to rotate this second plane and change its position vis-à-vis the original plane. There will be many more possible directions. What if you could bend this plane, not just rotate it further? The possibilities are endless! We can rotate such surfaces and superimpose them on top of each other, thus creating superimposed solids. This is what I mean by time expressed in space! Multidimensional.

The only problem is that we cannot feel or "see" it — because our bodies are our limitation. Our bodies live in three dimensions while we are physically here on Earth. The chemistry or physics in which we exist and live is focused on the three-dimensional space and a unidirectional timeline, not on multiple layers, planes and rotating, interpenetrating blocks, layers, or dimensions of time. Of course, we cannot function otherwise because due to our biology, we simply do not have such an opportunity.

MT: I can visualize what you mean by distinct dimensions, layers or planes of time. I like solids, spheres, and stereometry. I cannot fully grasp it in detail, but I have an overall idea. Please explain, though, what does this abstraction have to do with the music that I can hear?

HK: This multidimensionality of time is very important in composing a musical form. For example, there is an interesting clash of temporal layers in the genre of the opera. When I receive the text from the librettist, I notice that the writer has planned something and described it, working on the libretto from week to week. There is a plot and a dramatic structure, a temporal flow already encoded in the words. But when I get the written text, I start planning where the culmination and the concentration of musical events would take place. Then, if the librettist changes his mind and says that there must be some additional text, inserted due to his concept of drama, sometimes this request can and sometimes cannot be accommodated. Then, everything has to shift. The textual and dramatic climaxes are in different places. Occasionally, this extra text even has to be spoken, instead of sung, because there are too many words compared to the space allotted to the text by the music. In most cases, though, when such a problem arises, you have to add something musically, to create additional space for the text that's too long. I'm flexible enough to adapt: "Oh, we'll do this now, but then we'll extend it for a longer period of time." In general, I continually keep the overall temporal proportions of the music in my mind. These are the proportions that must be present in a composition for it to acquire a proper musical and dramatic flow.

When working with a text that has its own "encoded" structure of internal proportions, I have to adapt: "flexibility" is very important! However, this adaptation cannot go too far; it cannot result in a situation when the musical form breaks down and falls apart. It is not a rigid or unchanging form: it is not as if once I had planned these culminations, I could not change them at all. This is not the case. But there are limits. If the transformations go too far, then the spell breaks. Remember I told you about the listeners being in a "trance" while listening to the music? It is not good to present them with a rude awakening, when the temporal dimensions of text and music do not fit and clash. In such cases, it is the librettist who has to compromise and reduce the length of the text. Mostly, it is up to the composer. You have to adapt to make the finished composition make sense, musically and dramatically. The temporal dimensions have to be coherent.

MT: *Did you apply these considerations in your operas? The concept of "trance" or "spell" is quite applicable to your opera* The Mother of Black-winged Dreams *of 1995.*

HK: Let us leave details aside for the time being and focus on the conceptual framework in general. Dealing with two layers of time — verbal and musical — in the opera is quite similar to composing with temporal layers in instrumental music. Here, we have a square of time that is moving, and there we have various elements that are being combined to break its coherence. You have to be careful: some elements may fall in or out of the overall form. You can still use such elements in a very artistic way. You have to be open to these changes. In life, even if something comes up or something unexpected happens to you, you have to be ready for anything. Similarly, when composing, you need to be able to adapt and adjust. You have to always take the main principle into account, so that the whole musical organism holds together. You have to make sure while planning out and composing your work that the temporal form of your composition is very clear and that nothing, even poor execution, may disturb the flow of time. This is what I'm achieving now in my own works: even when a composition is not performed so well, even when there are errors made by performers, the whole thing, the temporal structure, is still there and holds the work together.

In performance, this hidden skeleton of temporal form is "transmitted" to the listeners to a greater or lesser degree, but it is always there. If this were not the case, the entire form would "shift" and would be bent out of shape, as it were, as soon as the interpretation failed. Imagine that the whole composition falls apart and the entire form immediately disintegrates if someone plays a section too slowly, or out of tune. It could happen only if it there were no clearly constructed proportions within the musical work. Everything would fall apart. But when I construct the entire piece and when I arrange it so that the music has a form consisting of multi-dimensional layers of distinct "types of time" — then the situation is different. Even if someone plays too slowly or misses something, it's still fine. In my music, there is always a hidden structure, there are always additional layers of coherence that would straighten out the flow and end the listeners' confusion. This concern for the overall structure of superimposed types of time serves my music well and it is one of its strengths.

MT: *I see, now I understand your comparison of listening to music to looking out the window on a train. Errors and confusions are in the foreground, and we see — or rather "hear" — this distant plan, this clearly articulated whole.*

HK: Yes. As I write, I actually think outside of music, because the temporal layers are there simultaneously and they are always present, whether you hear the individual layers, or not. This creates the continuity in the composition. My Piano Concerto is a good example of such conscious structuring of the polyphony of time.

MT: *In what way? Could you explain?*

HK: In the Baroque, many pieces begin with a slow

introduction; then, there is a gradual growth towards the climax, the acceleration to the top. In most cases, the piece ends in the fast tempo. It's different for me. I consciously compose my works from different "types" of time, as if the music consisted of several time layers or dimensions intersecting with each other, appearing and disappearing during the progress of the musical work. A given layer consists of a certain texture, of musical, harmonic and rhythmic phrases that have a constant, slowly changing tempo, a harmonic content, and a certain density. When a collision between these temporal layers, planes or dimensions occurs, we jump from one layer, one time dimension to another. We suddenly find ourselves in a stream of music with a different speed, density, and weight. And then we may experience another collision and a new intersection — a third layer appears, and maybe even a fourth one. But the previous temporal layers or dimensions do not disappear either. For now, they are "inaudible" and hidden, while constantly evolving and then, suddenly, coming to the fore...

From these collisions and transformations, a surprising course of the entire composition arises, emerging from a series of increasing tensions and resolutions, expectations and disappointments. In the process, to use my previous analogy of a turbulent flight, listeners may suddenly fall into a "hole" in the musical texture, which surprises them and maybe even scares them a little — such a sudden shift from one temporal layer to another may remind them of the moment when a plane suddenly falls 20-30 meters down during a blizzard... In the music, a surprising new temporal layer appears, and the musical action suddenly shifts into a new dimension of musical space-time. I like planning and creating these unusual experiences for my audiences and the musicians who play my music, like it too!

MT: *Thank you for introducing me to your musical world and a* *very original theory of multi-dimensional musical time. Your explanations clarify why in performance, your music provides the listeners with such haunting experiences.*

Edited and Translated from the Polish by Maja Trochimczyk

≈ MY PHILOSOPHY OF MUSIC ≈

Hanna Kulenty

Personal Essay to Accompany the Trumpet Concerto No. 3. Habilitation, Post-Doctoral Degree at the Karol Szymanowski Academy of Music in Katowice, September 2015

I am a Polish-Dutch composer.

I am a free creator from circa 1985, when I completed my compositional studies in Warsaw. Since 1992, I have also lived permanently in Holland. "Also" — because I have never emigrated from Poland and have no intention of ever doing so.

While leading my life in two countries, I link two cultures; I participate and function in two cultures, and not only in musical cultures. This extended functioning allows me to have a broader view of the world in general, as a whole: the world of music, the world of interpersonal relationships, and the world of human sensitivity.

This is also impacted by my rich artistic life and a very extensive compositional output. Since my music is being performed around the world, with each composition, with each performance, I acquire new experiences, new comparisons — a new freedom, detachment, and humility.

Exactly: these comparisons and artistic freedom, that luckily I was, have been, and still am able to maintain, allow me to be detached from reality. How important is it to feel such detachment? How important is it to be humble? How important is it to do what you want to do regardless of universally accepted fashions, or connections? How essential it is to be able to create!

Without humility, I would not have been able to get anywhere nor to reach my goals, while overcoming new challenges. Without respect for musical tradition (I will mostly discuss music here) I would have never been able to get anywhere at all. I would have been going round and round like a mouse running around a cylinder, I would have been lost in the dark corners of dying compositional techniques that have not always respected musical traditions....

How important it is to be able to focus on human sensitivity (in the general sense of this word) regardless of the geographic longitude and latitude where it is found.

How important it is to be able to focus on music: the music that grows from sensitivity and also this sensitivity causes...

Exactly: sensitivity and music. Sensitivity and emotions. Emotions and music. Music and physics? Is it all? Is it enough? And maybe, exactly, music and metaphysics?

Music is connected to sensitivity; at least it should be. And if it is connected to sensitivity, therefore it is also connected to emotions. We cannot ignore this. It is impossible. That's it. There is no music without emotions; there are no emotions without sensitivity (just as there is no money — the paper money — without its parity in gold, without the gold standard). There is no music without metaphysics.

In the 20th century, many efforts were made to stifle, eliminate emotions. Modernism was a denial of romanticism, where emotions really reached their zenith. On the one hand, it is difficult to be surprised by this — each exaggeration ends up in exhaustion, but, on the other hand, why reject everything? Why not maintain a balance? Why should we, while being tied up in the complicated knots of post-serial techniques and ultra-modernism, ridicule and reject what moves us?

It is as if I said to myself — from today on I will not eat, or I will not sleep, or I will never ever cry again... What a hypocrisy, what a lack of humility, respect. An error.

Why should we deny ourselves what we need? What is human? Why are emotion, beauty and goodness valued so low?

Why should we always destroy, so as to start again and reach the same conclusions and values? Is it not a loss of time? We would get much further by using "good energy" arising from the expansion of *cults and cultures.* Would we not get much further, if we evolve, and not continually struggle?

Because we will all "fit in" — all of us!

On the other hand, when looking at what we have reached, would we really, truly and completely be pleased with that?

Maybe not entirely... since music in the world has finally — and luckily —started to become more "musical" and touch in us, people, such strings that should be touched without any false shame.

A human being is built like a string. Yes a string, a "Pythagorean string" that can be divided into two, three, four, etc., parts, where the smaller is the numeric ratio, the more perfect — the interval.

The human cell is also the simplest and purest form of life. Everything can fit in there...

The spectra of all cells of a human being that result from their linear division after being arranged in a particular way create a certain whole. It is a "holy" whole, but only when we keep a certain holy order in the arrangement of all elements that collaborate with each other. Why a certain order? Because such an order implies a certain freedom, randomness (no two people are completely identical, unless they are clones). Such "holy" order has to be preserved under all conditions — also in the emotional sphere, and consequently, also in the spiritual sphere. If these conditions will not be fulfilled then a person will either be handicapped, damaged, or, in the worst case, that person would not be able to live, that person will die. We should remember about *this*. Also in music.

In music, if certain relationships and conditions will not be respected, this music will not be music at all but only a juxtaposition of sounds, without any rhyme or reason. This music will die a natural death without giving rise to emotions in its listeners, and only frightening them with its "bad energy," or, actually, with its lack of energy.

But how should we arrange these spectra and how should we put them together so that our human strings could resonate and start to move as well? How to preserve the order of "existence" of music on such a scale and in such proportions so as not to lose its "divinity"? So that the physics of the sound could also be its metaphysics?

For many years, I have been researching this issue and polishing my discoveries — as it turns out concerning not only my compositional technique. For years, my musical language has been evolving. Evolving also in its aesthetic form that results only and solely from my philosophy. Never the other way. I do not "play" with the sounds for the sake of sonority itself, and I do not apply to such games any smart theories. The sound is essential for me, to exemplify my visions that are not disturbed by any unwanted energy, or fashion.

However, it is important to adhere to some principles, needed to make new discoveries. First of all, it is essential to be humble, because only then we can listen to cosmos. We can listen to cosmos with our intuition. Let us give intuition a chance... Sooner or later, our brain will catch up to it and will verify its findings... Let us not be afraid of this process.

Let us also respect the holy order developed by cults and cultures. Let us keep the proportions that were developed over the centuries. Let us maintain respect, humility and equilibrium, but let us also be open and evaluate the past, while creating things that are new and fresh. Let us evolve and not *only* deny.

Let us experiment — by evaluating and trying out new techniques, new instruments, etc. But let us preserve ourselves and our sensitivity without being polluted by anything and anyone. Let us be faithful to our own philosophies. Let us strictly adhere to the rules and not strictly wander around the sphere of possibilities of our own imagination.

Let us approach with a beneficial attitude what seems to us un-logical — but we can realize it is logical, only it is beyond the reach of our brain, not fully used in 97%.

Let us not think that what seems to be is initially identified by the brain as not being, logical, cannot also touch upon the divine? Does it touch the divine, or not? Our awareness of this depends on our intuition and on our talent: both of them deserve our trust.

Therefore, let us connect the past with the future as much as we can and for good luck. Let us perceive the divine present. Let us extend this divine present by entering into its magic trance. This trance that is the measure of time and all its dimensions. Also, in music.

Exactly: music and time… music and trance… this also is inseparable.

≈ My Philosophy of Time ≈

Time and all of its Dimensions. If we speak of dimensions: let us consider *if and how* we can measure them, measure time.

Can we? Why does this extraordinary phenomenon give rise to so many emotions?

Plato thinks about it, Aristotle thinks about it, and other philosophers are hard at work, thinking, asking themselves questions that do not have simple, unequivocal answers. Plato clams that time emerged together with heaven, and heaven, according to Plato, has its beginning somewhere, sometime. Aristotle claims that all philosophers, with one exception, agree that time is eternal and its phenomenon, its essence, consists in the continuous motion. If there is motion — there is change — there is time. If there is no motion — there is no change — there is no time, because time doesn't exist without change and without motion. Only what should we do with these designations, "before" and "after"? Ah, yes, connect them with the present.

And while Aristotle was convincing us about the necessity of motion and change in order to obtain the definition of music and time (also musical time), Archimedes, in turn, considered musical time, as well as time in general, as a physical, experiential phenomenon, rooted in the natural order. Music is a phenomenon of the natural order.

Heraclitus from Ephesus, while not knowing how to capture the phenomenon of the flow of time, compared it to the flowing river. Isaac Newton taught that the absolute mathematical time flows by itself, in itself, independently from anything else. However, already Gottfried Wilhelm Leibniz claimed that time and space do not exist in the absolute sense, but are illusions.[1]

---

[1] Antoni Stańczyk, *Filozoficzne inspiracje w rozumieniu czasu muzycznego* [Philosophical Inspirations in the Notion of Musical Time]. Kraków: Musica Iagellonica, 2013. ISBN 978-7099-188-3, p. 49. Aristotle, *Dzieła Wszystkie. Fizyka-Księga* viii, 251b, [Complete Works. Physics. Book]. vol. 2 of *Complete Works*, translated into Polish by K. Lesniak, Warszawa: PWN, 1990.

We could continue to enumerate more and more names. However, if we look at this closely, then we realize that the first, and the second and the next philosopher are right. They are all right.

I consider each theory, in its own way, to be correct but incomplete. Am I the connection between them?

I want to see it *completely*. I want to feel and hear it completely.

That's why I pursue music: because music is, for me, the best, the fastest, and the most abstract, sensuous, and spiritual form of expression.

Music is my most comfortable language that I use to answer, or at least to try answering several of these key, existential questions.

Where is the beginning and the end of time? Why, in certain temporal areas, is time subject to perpetual motion that depends on the season of the year, night and day?

What impacts the initiation of different phenomena, their development and passing?

Can we stop time? Or maybe we can slow time down, especially when we are in the state of happiness — precisely in this state of the "divine present" (the present moment that lasts)? Or maybe we can accelerate time, when we are unhappy?

And maybe we are able to cross over certain zones of time that have their own rhythm, systematic organization, and a definite pulse? And maybe we are able to cross over the linear time, known as the fourth dimension (its definition was served to us by Einstein) and maybe we can transit into time's other, greater dimensions? And do this — let me say it this way — during our lifetimes?

What is this time in general and how many dimensions does it have? Because the fact that time has dimensions is certain. I am sure of it.

Regardless of which theory we accept, does time exist or does is not? Does time flow pure, unpolluted by anything, or does it flow only because of motion itself? Is time an illusion or not?

One thing is certain, as long as we exist, we do *notice* time. Moreover, we want to define it and measure it. If we did not exist, would it matter, whether time exists, or not? Because time could flow by itself, with any connection to our existence, whether we exist or not. Could it? Or maybe it would not flow by itself? However, if we do notice time, this means that time exists. But how? And maybe there are more times? Only we cannot know it yet? Do we guess? Are we seeking? I guess; I even know this for certain. I will try to prove it, first philosophically, and then musically, by describing one of my more recent works. But this will follow in a moment...

For now, some theory.

As we know there are four dimensions: length, plane, volume, and time. Let us call time T (from the initial of the word "time") and, more precisely, T^1. Why is it raised to the power of one? Because we live in a **linear** time, and not in a **planar** time, or a **spatial** time. (Is it certain we do not? Maybe we do?). We live in the linear time in this sense that human existence is programmed for linear time. Clearly, we are born and we die.

We cannot go back in time to our youth, and we cannot accelerate our natural old age. The musical tape or film tape can be played from the end to the beginning, but human life cannot be played backwards like that.

The musical time that the majority of us perceive also belongs to linear time. We listen to music from the beginning to end and even if we were to listen from the end to the beginning we still would have been listening in the order of the flow of seconds, in the biological rhythm of nature's clock. Our earthly nature. We would look at the watch and say, oh, about 20 minutes passed...

Here, musical events have their beginning and end.

The musical time, therefore, that time that we predominantly perceive, is a real time in which we live. Real, because linear. This is the fourth dimension. Music that we hear in real time of the fourth dimension is heard in space, but also our space, earthly space. Music flowing in real time of the fourth dimension also sounds in the third dimension called the volume. The fourth dimension sounds in 3-D.

Here, I will allow myself to make an observation.

A human being has two eyes and two ears. With the help of these organs functioning simultaneously and without any handicaps or challenges, a human being sees and hears in 3-D — that is, spatially, in volume, and not in 2-D, that is, within a plane. That could also have a logical explanation, since the function of two dimensions-parameters is the plane. Only if we cover up one eye we can see "planar-ly" that is, in two dimensions. If we cover up one ear, we can hear in a two-dimensional, "planar" way, that is, monophonically.

The 3-D space in which we see, hear, and function, and which we constantly try to improve and expand (what is well understood and unavoidable) will always be the 3-D space.

Following the path of these observations further, would it have been logical for us to have had not two but three eyes and three ears, to gain 3-D? Nonetheless, we have only a pair of eyes and a pair of ears, and our brain is this third force-parameter, this third connecting dimension.

So we can hear stereophonically, and such inventions as quadro-or-more-phony are only attempts to improve the quality of 3-D, aren't they?

On this occasion I would like to add, that I'm often puzzled by these observations — time, space, a different space, a better space, because we have dispersed instruments throughout the whole interior of the concert hall...

Do such discussions that lead us to consider whether we will really obtain a different, better space through a different placement of instruments in the hall, would simultaneously confirm the achievements of the other property of space, and through this the other reality?

Does some other space really exist, in *this* concept of our real world?

Actually, no. Such different space certainly cannot be attained in the real world, not in its literal sense and meaning. We may attain solely *its* enhanced quality; perhaps we would be looking around, perhaps the quality of sonorities would seem to us to be better, but this would not change the fact that space that is the third dimension is only and merely space—volume in which we are placed and in which the music is too. This music lasts from the beginning to the end in its linear time and existence. Consequently, whether better or worse in its quality, this 3-D would always be our, human and earthly 3-D. Another space surely cannot be attained in the real world. But in the *unreal* one?... Certainly.

Perhaps it is worthwhile to seek and attempt reaching beyond the human, real reality? At least *try* to do so?

Earlier I stated that musical time is perceived *predominantly* as linear time. Why do we predominantly perceive it as linear time, in its general meaning of the term? Because, the other, minority option is to perceive time and not only musical time as being raised to a power of... two, that is time squared — T^2 and the power of three, that is time cubed — T^3, and so forth.

And this *should not* be connected linearly with the earthly dimensions, in which these powers are also contained.

Those who perceive the following times T^2, T^3, and the times raised in higher powers, are *unfortunately,* still in the minority, because, firstly, human beings in their biological nature are not "in majority" or "predominantly" programmed and by that programming also not constructed for life in *other* times, and secondly, even if the brains of certain people have a greater "span" for the reception of the cosmos — in the so- called "flows" or "outbursts" of genius (what was, is and will be), the mass of average folks will equalize these differences...

Let us consider history. If such geniuses as Buddha, Christ or Muhammad were heard properly and ultimately to the end, we would not have had the Crusades, and maybe we even could have possessed the secret of eternity, and not only that. Our brains could have developed these unutilized percents, could have opened their "antennas" directed at other realities and other temporal dimensions. I think that teleportation would not have been a problem, as well as cellular changes that are necessary to complete passage from one dimension of time to another, for instance from T^2 to time raised to the power of three, four, five: T^3, T^4, T^5, etc. I will further expand on this subject in a moment...

At this time, I will allow myself to present my first thesis:

Whereas the linear time, that is the fourth dimension that we know and which we are, and that I shall call T, is a set of such subsets as the first dimension — of length, that I will call X, the second dimension — of surface/plane, that I will call XY, and the third dimension — of volume, that I will call XYZ, and whereas this results in such a relationship/parallel existence as XXY — XYZ — T, so therefore, the linear time to the power of one, that I will call the fourth dimension to the power of one, T^1, will be a set of such subsets as: the first dimension — of length to the power of one, that I will call X^1, the second dimension — of surface/plane to the power of one, that I will call XY^1, and the third dimension — of volume to the power of one that I will call XYZ^1, and this will result in the relationship of X^1 — XY^1 — XYZ^1 — T^1.

(Here I shall add that the terms "sets and subsets" are perhaps not perfect for my definition of temporal dimensions. I will use these terms based on a convention, because this usage is simply the most convenient).

The fact is that such a relationship certainly does exist. We live in time — the fourth dimension — in a linear fashion; similarly, we live in the other dimensions of length, plane and volume — the first, second and third dimension — also in a *linear* fashion. It is "linear" in a sense that we live on "earthly" conditions. It does not matter, that in its notation and earthly properties these dimensions are in the format of "raised to the power of." Our life, together with its earthly powers, is linear. Therefore, the relationship X — XY — XYZ — T is the *same* as the relationship X^1 — XY^1 — XYZ^1 and T^1.

Simultaneously, the subscript numbers that I added do not only help distinguish (and do it more visually than conceptually) the different, additional dimensions of time/times along with their "subsets" — this topic will be discussed shortly...

Therefore, this second thesis also pertains to other dimensions of time. This is a thesis that I profoundly believe in, deeply perceive and even attempt to name:

The relationship of time squared with its "subsets," that is X^2 — XY^2 — XYZ^2 — T^2, follows the same principles as the relationships of time to the power of free (cubed) with its own "subsets," that is $X^3 - X^3 - XYZ^3 - T^3$, and so forth.

If we assume that the linear time — T^1 is the *real* time, because we live in it, then the squared time — T^2, the cubed time — T^3, and the times raised to a higher power/or powers are *unreal* times because we do not live in these times (In general, we do not live in them)... Time raised to a power is therefore an unreal time in our human concept, but is it also non-existent?

Here, I have to express my doubts, because if I personally, in my own body, have perceived something more, this means that something more is happening. Something, that luckily has been perceived and will continue to be perceived not only by myself — myself alone — and not by myself as the first one, and nor by myself as the last one...

How is one to envision this unreal time in a general meaning of this notion?

In an altogether very simple way. Our Earth, our planet turns around its axis during each period of 24 hours. Thus, that one period of day and night always lasts 24 hours. Furthermore, the year lasts 365 days, because that is how long it takes for our planet to complete one rotation around the Sun.

If the speed of rotation of the Earth was accelerated or delayed (slowed down), that is, in either case, disturbed, all the temporal proportions would have changed. Theoretically we would have found ourselves in an unreal time, a time *non-belonging* among the properties of the Earth. Why theoretically? Because nobody and nothing on Earth would have survived this sudden disturbance of the forces of nature. However, if it somehow turned out that someone or something had survived such a sudden and intense temporal turbulence, the new time, perceived by that someone or something, would flow according to entirely different principles than those established earlier. It would flow slower or faster, but still in a linear fashion. It would have seemed as if we had been transferred to the orbit of Mercury, or Mars. Time flows faster or slower there in comparison to what we know on Earth; still, it flows in a linear fashion. Thus, the days or years have a beginning and an end. Only the mode of *how they exist* is entirely different. The unreal time may also be, as we have seen, a type of a linear time.

If the linear time T or T^1 that we know and perceive as real — on our planet — may also have been unreal, due to its placement beyond the borders of our planet — and if it again this time became real when we were transferred beyond the borders of our planet, therefore, the times T^2 and T^3 and so forth could also co-create such relationships. The times squared, cubed, T^2, T^3 and so forth, under earthly conditions could have been seen as completely unreal. Then they would have gained properties and characteristics of real times in the moment of their *identification and experience.*

How, then, can you identify the time that is squared or cubed, that is also an unreal time in the sense that it is not perceived by the majority?

And maybe it is real, because it is perceived by a minority? Still, "unfortunately" perceived only by the minority?

And maybe it is good that only some people can perceive this? Existential questions...

In any case I'm seriously considering whether it is certain that we live only and solely in the linear time? Do we not *also* live in the planar time, or spatial time?

≈ ≈ ≈

At least, we sometimes *happen to visit* the planar time or spatial time, don't we? How can we recognize that this is occurring in our earthly condition? How can we feel this unreality (as it were) while still *being alive*, during the span of our earthly life?

So, here' is my third thesis.

I think that we must:

First accept the principle that times squared (T^2) is a superimposition or the "plane" (function) of two different linear times, and the time cubed (T^3) is the superimposition or the "volume" (function) of three different linear times, and so forth.

Simultaneously, the linear times, that are times raised to the power of one (T^1) are superimposed on each other to create times T^2, T^3, and so forth. However, *also* the further dimensions of time — T^2, T^3, etc. — are superimposed on each other creating subsequent levels of powers and subsequent new dimensions of time. For instance $(T^2)^2$ or $(T^3)^2$, or $(T^2)^3$ or $(T^3)^3$, and so forth.

Therefore, once again:

First, we have to accept the principle that the superimposition on each other of at least two different types of time and not necessarily linear types of time will create its subsequent dimension (function, or power).

And then, we have to attempt to recognize, perceive and assimilate all that in such a way that the time that was hitherto *unreal* becomes *real*.

The trick is so that to feel or perceive those times *simultaneously*. Additionally, these times may be different. Long, short, or even. Theoretically the lengths of these times do not count, only (exactly and primarily indeed) their *functions*. We should intuitively perceive the functions of these times, the superimpositions on each other of times of different length, such as (let us use those as an example) the time of the Earth and the time of Mercury, or the time of the Earth, Mercury and Mars *simultaneously.*

Only this simultaneous perception of different times, and not necessarily linear times, gives us its different dimension. Its different plane, different volume, different power, and a completely different *space.*

In this moment, the word "space" acquires a new meaning. It is no longer congruent, as it was before, up to now, with the meaning of the concept of the "volume." The human volume...

Thus, we arrive at a space of different properties and a different reality. Additionally, this different/ new dimension of time that until now was an *unreal* time, at the moment of being recognized perceived and accepted became a *real* time. Thus, unreal time becomes real time when you *assimilate and recognize it.*

Simultaneous perception of these temporal superimpositions (not necessarily of different length) may also be — and also is — perceived in music.

The same times are perceived in music because human beings create music. Humans create music that contains different dimensions of time/ times on condition that humans are able to *recognize and perceive* these other times, other dimensions.

There could be also a possibility that the music that contains different dimensions of time will possess the human being? I cannot exclude such a possibility because I myself am involved in this subject practically from birth. It is not important what is first — the egg, or the chicken. It is important that I accept the theory of time to the power of... This theory was almost imposed on me. So therefore I set up my "antennas" to the cosmos and with humility try to accept these waves.

I write music, I try to write music that is the function of several times, for instance the times of the Earth, Mercury or Mars (as I had earlier conventionally named them) and this is (as it were) "less terrifying." (I will explain this later).

But I also write music with the function of times of even durations. The function of several times of even — linear and therefore "human" length. The music with the function of times of different human life-spans. I perceive different human lives simultaneously and this is — let me say it — "more terrifying" even though it is possible to accept and to perform that task.

Let me explain:

To put it simply, if you "cheat" or brains and if you shift *also* into a different span of time, for instance a 36-hour time span of one day and night (not necessarily lasting as long as on Mars….), then, after a certain period of time your organism will become habituated to a different reality and finally it will get used to it, so you will accept it. The present, that is the connection between the past and the present will be *extended.*

Additionally, if you will not lose the good, and *only* good energy, this extended present will be an extended happiness. Nirvana. In the end, we seek to extend happiness and not to shorten it, don't we?

Therefore, longer times will also be "more attractive," because *there* we also age much slower. Would then the good energy, increasingly better energy, divine energy be able to slow down or even t stop the earthly friction?

Simultaneously, we *also* live in the 24-hour rhythm of the day, because that is how it is with us. That's it. We get up in the morning; we go to sleep at night.

If we succeed in maintaining the function of these two times while living in one and experiencing the other, it is good. If we succeed in maintain the function of three times or more, not necessarily linear times, it is still better. Additionally, the larger times (linear and not only linear) give us not only a longer present in which if (as it were) we take care of things well, our sense of h happiness will also be extended. The longer times give us a better sense of detachment and of balance. In this perceive of a longer life, we will first and foremost improve its quality and value.

Let us, then, remain in the divine present, in its trance; in the present that truly is the most important. Let the moment last (this is the "less frightening" function of different times).

However, if we, in turn, "cheat" our brain in the sense that we allow our "antennas" receive *different* waves, we cannot exclude the possibility that we can thus contact the waves of other beings?

Perhaps human beings that had lived earlier? Or that will live? And maybe those that had lived, are alive now, and will live — simultaneously?

It is hard to imagine this, but on the other hand I did not invent such notions as that of ghosts, life after life, reincarnation or *déjà-vu*. So, if I perceive the functions of different linear times, different human lives, while living in the year 2015 and seeing simultaneously events from the year 1926, for instance, I can only be happy about it.

I am happy that I do not only live, but also *participate* in a time that is, for instance, squared or raised to higher powers. (This is the more "terrifying" aspect of my ability to perceive times "to the power of...").

One thing is certain, in music it sounds *similar.*

Therefore, while writing music, while writing my philosophy in sounds, while seeking in these sounds the reflection of my feelings, perceives and thoughts, I try to write music using longer times as well as those "extra-terrestrial times" (rather than the "beyond the grave times")...

I try to reach such a trance that will allow us to feel this other, or several other "present-s". The happier presents. I try to write music that contains different times and their different dimensions.

Simultaneous perceived different universes that nonetheless will be performed *here and now*.

And when after the completion of the work, I or we will wake up from the trance and we'll say — "Oh, my, how long was that, twenty minutes? Impossible I felt it was much shorter" — this will be for me the signal that *all* of this works. That all *this* is a *truth* and an attempt of extending, stopping the present will be an attempt of touching eternity.

One more theory — reflection, entirely unconnected to music, but clearly linked to time:

Everything that so beautifully is reborn each spring (here I'm speaking about Nature) dies again in the fall, doesn't it. Does it? Actually, not. If something really died, it would not have been born again. So that we people also do not die as well and do not die for real, because we can be reborn. And even though we are not immediate witnesses of that we are being seen by nature.

As we see the nature being reborn, so the nature also sees us being reborn — us people. And if nature "has no idea" about the fact that it is being reborn, why should we comprehend the fact of our own rebirth?

We are, despite everything, a part of nature, a part of the living world .It is so obvious for us to see that nature is being reborn. How obvious it is for nature to "see" that we are being reborn. Let us trust nature. Let us trust the living world. I did.

≈ My Compositional Techniques ≈

Before I start describing my Trumpet Concerto No. 3, I would like to briefly outline my compositional path to the moment where I find myself now, while writing this work. In my Master's Thesis from 1985, entitled *Plurality in Unity, or the Way of Organizing Great Times,* I defined my first technique, that I later called the "Polyphony of Arcs."[2]

In general, I defined the "Polyphony of the Arcs" in the following way:

"[...] Through the plurality, that to the strongest extent allows the superposition on each other of different energetic layers, different climates, that is different arcs — since individual musical layers would have such a diagram of an arc — I achieve a certain type of formal polyphony. A multiplication of the form. This polyphony refers not only to the way of organizing sound material by itself (texture, aesthetics, what is possible but not essential) but precisely to the way of organizing of the whole work. This whole is a form that is a set of several arcs unfolding at the same time. Moreover, these arcs have to be constructed in such a way that after their eventual separation they could each create a separate work. In this moment, the focus is not the richness of the sound material, but rather the development of the musical dramaturgy in itself.

---

[2] Hanna Kulenty: *Plurality in Unity, or the Way of Organizing Great Times,* essay component of the Master's Thesis, complementing the Master's Thesis in composition, written under the supervision of Prof. Włodzimierz Kotoński, Warsaw: F. Chopin Academy of Music, January 1986. Typescript in the holdings of the Library of the F. Chopin University of Music, Warsaw, Poland.

The plurality of narrative plots in the form, the plurality of these formal arcs will, independently of the possible polyphony of layers in each individual arc, create the whole composition — as being, in a certain sense infinite and not closed in its psychological perception [...]."

Why will this form be in a certain sense infinite and not closed?

Because the predictability connected to the clarity of form to which we are accustomed in the 20th century — will be disturbed.

This means that, for instance, in modernism where music in general flows in accordance to the principle of "action — reaction" we are generally capable of foreseeing how the work will develop and when we will be able to relax our senses and intellect for a moment of rest before the subsequent moment of "tension." Similarly, in minimalism, when the work follows the designated course, flowing in waves, we may either positively immerse ourselves in these waves, or even "drown" in them. However, in my music this flow will not be so obvious.

Therefore, the typical predictability of form does not exist in my music; instead, it is the predictability based on the principle of seeking catharsis — this can be found here, indeed.

I will say more — this is my goal, just as my goal is stopping, or to be even more precise, *extending* the present — and as follows — "extending" time.

While writing music in the technique of "the polyphony of arcs" (but not only in that technique) I typically overwhelm my listeners with energy on the borderline of endurance, so as to "lessen the tension" only in the logarithmic point of this accumulated form. The logarithm of the polyphony of arcs.

The logarithm of the polyphony of growing temporal-spatial lines.

In my Master's Thesis we continue to read:

"[...] The tension arising between individual layers is the greater the less comprehensible is the clash, juxtaposition of these layers with each other and a seeming lack of logical consequence — in the understanding d of tension, drama, that of course exists, but as if beyond the framework of the composition.[...]"

True, this seeming lack of consequence in the understating but not in the *perception*. Here arises the very important, if not the most important, task for a composer: to balance the tensions between individual arcs. The definition of their proportions — to what extent these arcs can be independent of each other and abstract in their relationships, and to what extent they can be understandable, legible and easily assimilated by the listener. The first listener — that is myself, the composer (here also I have to trust nature).

In my doctoral dissertation of 2012, entitled *New Aspects of Using my Technique of Temporal-Spatial Polyphony in the Composition* **E-Motions** *for Accordion, Strings and Percussion*, I summarized my first composition technique in the following way: [3]

"[...] It is necessary to remember about balanced, easy-to-assimilate dramaturgy of a work (the whole of the form) independently of its *complexity* and polyphony, so that after crossing a certain perceptual limit chaos does not ensue.[...]"

---

[3] Hanna Kulenty, *New Aspects of Using my Technique of Temporal-Spatial Polyphony in the Composition* **E-Motions** *for Accordion, Strings and Percussion*. Doctoral dissertation, complementing Doctoral Work in Composition, written under the supervision of Prof. Grażyna Pstrokońska-Nawratil. Wrocław: Karol Lipiński Academy of Music, 2012. Typescript in the Library of the Karol Lipiński Academy of Music, Wrocław, Poland.

Therefore, in my music I do not "relent" in the moments when we would wish for me to do so, just because we have been used to it, or because we had decided to think that way and follow the construction. In contrast, I "pile up" — I stretch without a breather all these layers, arcs, or what I call them now — temporal-spatial lines — while remembering, of course, about the most perfect (in my perception) proportions of dramaturgy and not only of dramatic narrative.

I emphasized this statement, "not only dramatic narrative" because not only drama-related proportions are important.

What is also significant are (what I call) the "cellular" proportions that rely on the balance in organizing sound material in each of its cell. Thus, the structure of the sound/sounds, with the preservation of the order of spectrum, the sound texture, harmony, rhythm, instrumentation, and so forth.

In short —— all the elements that allow reaching such energy of music that I need to achieve certain emotions and a psychological-physiological state in the listener.

Because this emotional state of a listener after listening to my work, or rather his/her "transposition" ("ascension") to the other dimensions of time is for me the overriding principle, I do not focus primarily (in this work) on my compositional workshop. As I had mentioned earlier — my aesthetics, and therefore my compositional workshop — are the consequence of my philosophy, and not *vice versa*.

My "compositional kitchen" will be revealed here to the extent it will be necessary for me to describe the Trumpet Concerto No. 3. Besides, and luckily so, music can be heard…

In my doctoral dissertation, where I attempted to summarize my technique of "Temporal-spatial Polyphony" we read further:[4]

"[...] The principles of the new technique are almost the same as the principles of the "Polyphony of Arcs," but my discoveries in the area of temporal-spatial from the past ten years are so significant, that the linear and horizontal shapes of these arcs has been replaced by a more conscious, mature and more adequate for these discoveries "round" vision (form) of spatial-temporal lines that do not, as much, permeate each other, as they exist side by side. [...]"*

What does this mean?

This means, first of all, that the "Polyphony of Arcs" has been in a natural way replaced by a new technique that I keep discovering and that I allowed myself to spontaneously name "Temporal-spatial Polyphony."

Secondly, the lines — arcs that I had been using, are now rounded Visions (forms) of different times. Why rounded? Because temporal-spatial lines lose their linear shape by connecting the proverbial beginning with the proverbial end. By doing so, they create the shape of the circle, and, as follows also the two-dimensional flat circle on the plane and a sphere.

This means, thirdly, that the times that I perceive and that I try to visualize in my music and with my music, have the shapes of linear circle, planar circle, and a sphere.

Therefore:

The linear time (T^1) will have the shape of a linear circle, the squared time (T^2) will have the shape of a planar circle, and the cubed time (T^3) will have the shape of a sphere, an "elastic" sphere.

---

[4] Hanna Kulenty, *New Aspects*, 2012, *op. cit.*

Time raised to greater powers will organize solely the space of the "spherical shape" of time, of its proportions and dimensions in the realm (generally speaking) of macro- and micro-cosmos.

Therefore, whether it will be the expansion of the universe, or its contraction and increasing density — on the principle of black holes — or whether it will be the expansion and contraction on the principles of "microscope-telescope," this is all very similar, logically, and inseparably. To breathe out, you have to breathe in. To have energy, there must be anti-energy. Black-white, yin and yang, etc.

At the end, this does not matter much, in which direction we go, does it? Whether we go to the right or to the left? The end will be the beginning and the beginning the end. The linear circle will be a circle, the planar circle will be a circle on the plane, and a sphere will be a sphere.

"[...] Therefore after writing several dozen of works in the technique of "Polyphony of Arcs" — in the 1980s and the first half of the 1990s, in the past century — I started to think about what could happen if I have given up the plurality of these layers, arcs, etc., and if, instead, I focused only on one, two or three arcs at the most, while "stretching" them to the limits of perception?

I decided to take this risk. I momentarily gave up the form I knew well and felt safe using, that is my well-tested compositional technique (analyzed by many musicologists around the world) and I started to write new music that I called "European trance music."

Why?

Because it was my trance, because it was Polish-Dutch, and therefore European. "European Trance" — the 1990s and the beginning of the 21st century.

It was quite a challenge, because I started to be compared to composers of minimal music. I have nothing against minimalism but beyond several similarities of (only and exclusively) a purely aesthetic nature, there was nothing more in common. A completely different dramaturgy. Of course, there are repetitions, obsessive ostinati, but.... What about the music for instance of the Far East, does it not contain ostinati? Are we going to call this music "minimal" as well? Thus: obsessive ostinati. Only why? To what purpose?

That is why: to reach this different time... And through trance perceive at least for a moment this other, magical time-space. So that through trance you could touch even just for a moment the metaphysical, that something that cannot be precisely named in words. Trance... But how to reach it, how to control it? How to convey, simultaneously, what is given to us, to me, to be conveyed?

How to convey this in an ideal way?

Would time squared, time cubed be an attempt to answer that? [...]"[5]

It could be.

Actually, it is my conviction that it could be, because it was, is and will be. I am certain of this.

This is why do I spill so many notes onto the music paper, and so many words on the paper of this essay, that is, clearly, a continuation of my research/quest. This is yet another attempt to name my discoveries made in the whole span of my life, up to the present moment.

---

[5] Kulenty, *New Aspects*, 2012, *op. cit.*

"[....] The physical perception of time to the power of... descended upon me during the writing of my second opera, *Hoffmanniana* in 2001.

Perhaps just the theme of the opera — seven selected days from the life of E.T.A. Hoffmann and seven days from the life of Andrei Tarkovsky, intertwined — one in the chronological order (Hoffmann) and the other one from the end backwards (Tarkovsky) influenced me to literally see a vision of this different time-space?

Maybe I matured to this in my (clearly) multi-year research? Perhaps this was impacted by my very strange dreams, and, actually, a different, *parallel* reality that I had experienced at the time?

The fact is that after my enthusiastic retelling of these discoveries to people whom I could trust, the majority commented about it by comparing my theory to the physical string theory. (Honestly speaking, I have never before heard about the string theory, nor was ever interested in it).

My visions presented parallel and independent times, initiated as if were from the same source and flowing each in its own direction. I could compare these bunches of times to the image of a bunch of New Year's balloons on strings or wires that I remember from my childhood. These strings or wires were stuck in something round and solid (a cabbage, celery, or a big potato, etc.) and were waving in the wind... Interestingly, the closer they were to the round solid, the better was the attraction and feeling of vibrations of these balloon wires and, what follows, a better attraction and perception of these different temporal lines.

To put it simply, I could feel several lives simultaneously, with a certain, appropriate setting of my *antenna.*

I did not want to enter into and immerse myself in the physical secrets; instead, as soon as possible I wanted to translate my discoveries into a musical language. Therefore, by using the example of my Piano Concerto No. 3 (2003-2004) I realized these temporal-spatial lines ("[...] — today — circles, planar circles, and spheres" [...]) with a minimal differentiation of musical material in such a way, so as to clearly perceive these differentiations and simultaneously preserve the continuity of the phrase, the continuation of trance. For instance, playing very fast musical passages on black keys of the piano, and suddenly starting to play the same passages on white keys.

What is important is that the continuity of trance is preserved (it must be preserved) and that the clearly perceived structural-sonic "turbulences" should only suggest any and all emotional changes. Temporal-spatial changes. [...]"[6]

≈ My Current Compositional Technique ≈

Just so — musical turbulences, is a good description of music that I compose today. Harmonic turbulences, including bitonality; rhythmic turbulences; changes of tempi and meters, etc., that exist beside each other (successively), or that are superimposed on each other — time-space turbulences; *spatio-temporal* turbulences and surrealism — this is my calling card. This is music that has so far endured and developed from the beginning of the 21st century to the present moment.

In all, I am the author of over one hundred compositions for different musical ensembles — from solo instruments, through chamber ensembles, symphony orchestra, as well as opera, ballet, theater and film music. With few exceptions, all of my compositions have been and are being performed on almost all continents; the majority of them are performed repeatedly. Wherein, each composition is different. Each

---

[6] Kulenty, *New Aspects*, 2012, *op. cit.*

work possesses — as it were — a different net or map, placing the different times together. Sometimes it happens that a very well designed and well-functioning net/map is attractive and seductive enough so that I use it in several subsequent compositions. Why? Simply because I want to further "play" with these times, giving them an opportunity to resound in different constellations, such as, e.g. different instrumental settings. One is certain, however (luckily); it is also commonly shared and gradually more and more prefect: the trance that is created by my music takes us into a different reality. Into a reality of "longer/extended" times, where *the present time* is extended as well (and first of all). Therefore, we perceive the piece to be of much shorter duration, than it is in reality. In a certain sense, our brains are cheated, manipulated and hypnotized. It is transitioned and transitions into a different time in such a discreet way, that we do not even notice it happening. This is very important. Let me explain…

A long time ago, during the music courses in Darmstadt, I had an opportunity to participate in the performance of the Second String Quartet of Morton Feldman. The Kronos Quartet played and my job was to turn the pages for the second violinist. Each musician of the quartet had a girl-assistant assigned to turn the pages. This is what the composer decreed; Feldman even picked us personally. At the beginning, I was surprised that a quartet needs as many as four page-turning assistants, but when I sat down with the musicians for the performance, my doubts evaporated very quickly.

This work lasts for over four hours — without an intermission, and any breaks in the flow of the music. The very slow notes, that mostly without greater changes attempted to pull us into a state of the trance, initially did not do their tasks very well. From the corner of my eye, I saw how people were leaving the hall quietly, one by one. I would certainly have left too, had I been seated in the audience. Because I could not do it, I survived to the end.

My transition into trance took place after about twenty minutes.

In the meantime, I went through a phase of powerlessness, rage and laughter, while watching some people return to the hall with... a beer. After twenty minutes I "floated away"... and after the completion of the performance I sat there, hypnotized, similarly to a handful of people, left in the concert hall.

My conclusion was immediate.

There is Someone, who (also) wants to stop time. This is good, This is very good, but why not attempt to find a more *universal* way of enchanting people, and not only those select few? What should be done to not discourage, but instead encourage?

This question was bothering me for many years and I could answer it only when, firstly, I acquired an extensive compositional technique, and, secondly, I experienced all these theories of time: I perceived different times in my own life, in my own body...

Another example: films by Tarkovsky.

While composing my opera *Hoffmanniana* based on a screenplay by Andrei Tarkovsky, I regularly went to the cinema to watch his films. An obvious thing to do. In this case, I also noticed people, who after several or several dozen minutes into the film projection, were leaving the hall, while those who remained until the end of the film were seating hypnotized.

The "long" times, "extra-terrestrial" times started at the beginning and lasted until the end of the film. (This is the same principle as in the Second String Quartet by Feldman). We watch, for instance in *Nostalgia,* a scene where a person tries to walk thorough an empty swimming pool with a burning candle. If the candle is extinguished before reaching the other edge of the swimming pool, the activity has to be repeated. "What an action" — I think to myself while simultaneously I begin to be pulled into this trance. The candle burns out prematurely and the person must again go back, light the candle, and start walking again. And this is done several times, until the task is completed. This section of the film lasted for maybe twenty minutes, maybe for more.... Not important. In this moment, the flow of time *stopped* and the director could do whatever he wanted with his audience. It is not important, what action is represented, whether there is any action at all, is it? How much time has passed? How many minutes of our life we have set aside for this film – so very precious minutes, cherished by each film director, who typically has too few of these minutes at his disposal?

I became aware that this sequence is like a scene from life. A film depicting a scene from life — in a one to one representation. But film is not life and typically in film action is greatly accelerated. Nonetheless, had we wanted to depict several years from a human life in the form of one to one film, we would have needed a film that would have lasted for several years. The conclusion arises immediately:

Art is mostly an accelerated version of the image of life and times; "long" times that logically should be called "extra-terrestrial/unreal" times in art, are to a greatest possible extent "earthly/real" in life. And *vice versa*, the "earthly/real" times of life acquire features of "extra-terrestrial/unreal" times, for instance in film, because who would endure a performance that lasts for several days?

The *impossibility* to perform or *difficulty to perform* endows works of art with the characteristics of "extra-terrestrial/unreal."

Whatever the way I look at it, I continually reach the same conclusion, as if I were running around a circle, or a planar circle, or around a sphere:

Whether in music, or in life — "longer" times impact an extended perception of the present and entering into the state of trance. This trance, in turn, is the connection to the transition into a different, extended reality.

What do I do, so that to stop time in my music, so as to "enchant" people — not only those select few, but also all those... impatient ones?

I try to introduce a more universal way of "hypnotizing" the audience, by encouraging them to remain in the hall, and not discouraging them at all.

This does not mean, however, that I write "for the public" though theoretically what could have been wrong with it? Maybe that I would then have to adjust to the tastes and levels of others. No, this is not so. I do not adjust to the level of others; but I still have a full awareness of the "biological" makeup of the human being, of his/her physiology, intuition, sensitivity, etc. So, I try to respect this, while simultaneously seeking to bring closer, and convince them about, the value of my discoveries. Ultimately, I consider myself a creator.

While writing music, I write first and foremost for myself. I am my own first listener and I know the best that if my own organism is able to stand and withhold this type of tension that will allow me to enter the state of trance and perceive different dimensions of time, so other people will perceive this, too. Of course, not everyone, and not to the same extent; this is an issue of individual characteristics of each particular human being.

In any case, I do what I am supposed to, while being aware of the fact that my music works the way it is supposed to work, the way it should work. And I am very happy when I succeed in reaching my goals.

While preparing the net-map of my times in a musical composition, I *never* start from "long" times (the so-called "extra-terrestrial" ones). I decide to lead the listener into trance gradually, discreetly and unnoticeably, while starting my composition always in an "earthly" type of time that I call "short or conventional" time. Simultaneously, this "short" time does not always mean that the music is fast, and "long" time is not always associated with slow music. For the most part, the "short" time may be and mostly is a characteristic of fast music, and the "long" time is typically associated with slow music, but this is subject to a *different* scale of comparisons.

Therefore, if at the beginning of the work I write slow notes, slow music, this does not mean that I write in a time that is "extra-terrestrial" or "long." No, not yet.

Slow music *does not necessarily* belong to slow — "long" times. It also may belong primarily to "conventional" or "short" times. It is the case, because tempo is not the only factor that impacts this classification. It is also affected by the *way of narrating* music, the way of arranging musical events in such a way that this music starts to *escape* beyond human, conventional perception.

Here, we start momentarily to lose control, because something begins to happen to us that are quite strange. On the one hand, we cease to comprehend music that was up to this moment unfolding and comprehensible. On the other hand, our curiosity and the trance that has already started to work within us invite us to enter into a different reality. The whole secret consists in maintaining such a balance that the music that has not been comprehensible becomes comprehensible in the sense that during the transition from the "Earth orbit" to the "Mars orbit" (I use these terms as an example, see the beginning of this essay), we do not fall into an abyss...

Music is a set of acoustic events that are arranged in a particular, and not in any other, fashion and that impact our senses and souls — this is very significant and maybe even the most significant.

Regardless whether this music is slow or fast, if we perceive music in a comprehensible way, that is, if its perception is not disturbed — our brains are happy, our souls are happy, and we are moved by it... This means that our time is congruent with the time of the flow of music. Our "earthly-real" time is congruent with the "earthly-real" time of the flow of music.

The "conventional" time, from which I commence each work and continue it through about 9 to 12 minutes, is a type of time that I seek to *preserve* or *secure* with such a set of sounds, such a *theme* of music, such music, that will be for the listener, in a certain sense, easily recognizable — because it will be friendly towards our senses, and through that, it will be *expected*, whether consciously or not. After that, I can start "enchanting" people with the temporal dimensions the way I want to, and for as long as I want to.

Here, I would like to note that all post-serial, modernist techniques do not work in practice. Our human hearing, our senses, even our brains are not capable of capturing and remembering so many events, that in a natural way could have been transformed from "short" into "long" times, that have been logically invented and developed by us on paper, but that (unfortunately) would lose its power in reality.

This means that we can perceive such music "in a human way," in a "conventional" time, but this mode of perception is much more intellectual than sensual.

Due to the fact that music is perceived more intellectually than sensually, we lose the possibility of a greater mobilization of intuition, which, as it is well known, is always the stimulus for invention. For it is the brain that should be catching up to the intuition, and not the other way around.

I know what I'm talking about, because for over thirty years I could test this myself. I could have continued to write in such a way as I was writing 25 years ago until today, but what for?

≈ ≈ ≈

Such music would never allow me to transition to "longer" times, due to its *invented* construction, invented by a human being. Invented and therefore limited and limiting in construction. Invented... I doubt whether ultimately perceived.

Therefore, I emphasize one more time how important it is to have respect for tradition, for developed models, for the culture, cult, and nature. The years of practice, years of intellect catching up to intuition... these only make us masters...

My task as a creator is a *fluid* transitioning of a listener from the "short- conventional" times to the "long" times, and then leaving the listener in this "hypnosis," this trance for as long as I consider it appropriate.

First of all, I attempt to do it to myself — as my own first listener. The so-called "short" times (generally speaking) are intertwined with each other and superimposed on each other based on the principle of arcs — similarly to my previous compositional technique. Ultimately, these times are superimposed on each other and permeate each other in the forms of linear circles, planar circles, and spheres.

As I had mentioned earlier, after about 9-12 minutes into the piece a moment occurs when I begin to slow down the musical narration. This is the moment to start expand our perception, our present time and this time, that is, as it is shown, a "relative" phenomenon. The work may last for as long as almost an hour and we will not even feel that.

In each composition, as I had earlier mentioned, this process occurs in a different way, but in accordance with similar principles.

Sometimes, it is so that I need more time for the "earthly" time because the music is arranged in such a way. Sometimes, I intertwine and "smuggle" the time that is "extra-terrestrial" earlier (as in the case of **E-Motions**, described in detail in my doctoral thesis), because that is what the music wants. This is what I want.

I would describe this in one sentence that captures my activity in general. It should be defined as follows:

I present a musical action or musical actions, and subsequently show these musical actions in a decelerated tempo, and, if necessary, I even stop them.

I could compare this to the recording of a certain event by a film camera. We capture the action and then we analyze it and distill into elemental factors all the way down to (even) complete stopping of the image. For instance, we can see a person in a store, someone who steals something and escapes. We want to see more details, so we watch this image projected slower and slower; the slower we watch it, the more details we can notice. Finally, we stop the image and stare into this "microcosm."

Precisely...

Staring into the microcosm or macrocosm? Staring through a microscope or a telescope?

What is first and what is last? What is the beginning and what is the end? And is it important, or maybe it does not mean that much, what would be the order of events?

I do my own thing by connecting the beginning to the end. Or maybe the other way around? I do not know... But I do know one thing that I have to be doing this, and that's it.

≈ ≈ ≈

Trumpet Concerto No. 3
For Trumpet and Symphony Orchestra

This composition was written in 2014 for Marco Blaauw and the orchestra NOSPR.

The premiere took place on 17 April 2015 during the Festival of Premieres in Katowice, Poland.

In the program we read the following:

"[...] This piece has been written using the technique of "Temporal-spatial Polyphony" and it represents yet another version of my experiments with time and time-space. While preparing the listener to a gradual transition into different – "longer" — times, I initially present to them the so-called "short" times — the "conventional" music, that is, a music that contains such interesting musical action and that is so physiologically friendly to us, humans, that it holds us in suspense. Then, I present "longer" times and, to put it simply, I gradually lead the listeners into trance. I "hypnotize" them by showing some fragments heard earlier in what I call "slow motion." Finally, I slow down the music to such an extent, that its natural, nearly physiological stoppage — or fading out — is both expected and inevitable. This happens through a manipulation of our perceptions, and not only of "spatio-temporal" characteristics [...]"[7]

In the case of the Trumpet Concerto No. 3, the "short — conventional" time is a slow, simple melody of the trumpet presented at the beginning of the work, with a modest accompaniment of the piano and delicate colors of the orchestra. This melody is gradually "mistuned' as it were — through heterophonic processes, in which selected wind instruments gradually become a kind of an echo to the leading melody of the solo trumpet, while the heterophonic glissandi in the first and second violins are an extension of— the percussion or *vice versa*, and the flageolets in the reminder of the string instruments are, as it were, the decelerating echo of the accompaniment of the piano.

In short, there is this melody, which, in general, functions in a bizarre way. First of all, it does not lead to any resolutions (releases) of harmony, of a cadential type, to which we are accustomed in the major/minor system. Instead, it shifts in a stepwise motion, moving gradually downwards or upwards, though in a different way. Here, I will allow myself to remind my readers of the definition of this type of ascending and descending harmonies as "harmonic turbulences." Secondly, this melody starts gradually to slow down while simultaneously accelerating. Actually, its whole instrumental "halo" begins to decelerate, that is, all these heterophonic echoes.

This process lasts for about 4.5 minutes and exactly in this moment the preparation commences for the transition into the "long" times. Theoretically, I could already be transitioning into "longer" times, but I am not doing this yet.

---

[7] Hanna Kulenty, **Trumpet Concerto No. 3** for trumpet and symphony orchestra (2014). Program Notes from the Festival of Premieres (Festival prawykonań) in Katowice, Poland, 17 April 2015, Marco Blaauw - trumpet, National Symphony Orchestra of the Polish Radio, Alexander Humala — conductor.

Still, not doing this. For one, simple reason: four minutes is for me *too little* to enter into a trance. Such a trance, as I had planned for this composition.

The melody therefore seems to be "suspended" — in the sense that the piano accompaniment is accelerated by one third of the initial tempo (from 64 to 96 quarter-notes per minute), thus suggesting to us a transition into a faster action and also a faster "short" time, that could be a different "short time," or a continuation of the previous "short" time. In turn, the echo of the piano accompaniment that is the flageolets by strings clearly decelerates and this suggests to us a transition into a slower time — a "longer" time. This gives us a strange sense of being divided — we seem to be petrified in expectation of the "long" times and simultaneously wait for the "short " times. Then, the curiosity about the eventual action of the music itself, the development of its phrasing and dramaturgy, suggested by the "short" time — wins. The melody, suspended on (as it were) a dominant-seventh chord that is never resolved, then passes into a very fast tempo and a very dynamic action, that in a moment will be subject simultaneously to an acceleration and a deceleration... But this will happen in a moment.

For now, we are in the border of two "short" times, where the first was a tranquil, simple melody and the second is an obsessive, chromatic theme, repeated in different melodic, rhythmic, harmonic, agogic, and instrumental configurations.

Here, the initial tempo is suddenly doubled (64 to 128 quarter-notes per minute). We do not perceive any especially distinct acceleration because we find ourselves, as if we were "on the run" in the following, fast musical action.

This fragment lasts without interruptions for about five minutes. This is "short" time that evolves and, generally speaking, gradually accelerates; however, there are attempts of "stretching" this "short" time into a "longer" time by using unexpected augmentation of themes and motives, which however, quickly return to their basic track.

More or less after the ninth minute of the work the "short" time starts to slow down, transitioning naturally into a "longer" time, but (what is paradoxical from the logical point of view) the music then starts to accelerate.

The unexpected accelerando appears — through the change of tempo by one third in comparison to the previous tempo (128 to 192). The motives — themes that were remembered and recognizable from the earlier fragment are now presented in augmentation, whereas the orchestral accompaniment (particularly the strings) speeds down in a neck-breaking tempo. Besides, the theme of the trumpet is also subject to acceleration at the end of this section of the composition that creates a culmination for the whole work.

Near the fourteenth minute of the piece, the "short" time, that occasionally was becoming a "longer" time (and thus was liberating these "longer" times), begins to gradually slow down, so that it ultimately becomes a "long" time for good. And to the extent that it is possible and necessary, it continues to lengthen during the continuation of the piece.

As I have written earlier, in general after more or less 9 to 12 minutes, I typically start to "enchant" my listeners... In the case of this Concerto, the "magic" starts after the 14th minute. This is *precisely this* moment, when I start leading the listeners into trance. A type of trance that I had planned for his particular composition. A trance that lets the listeners be hypnotized with the magic of another present another time-space.

Here, for yet another time, appears the melody of the trumpet, well-known earlier, coupled with a modest accompaniment of the piano and the "mistuned" orchestra. The melody that is perceived in this moment to be maintained in the "long" time. Why? Because after a fast action and a very fast tempo of the music, we need a moment of reflection. A kind of a "logarithm" of what we have heard before. And this will not be disturbed for us by a simple melody; in fact, it will strengthen the effect.

Finally, the "long" time starts to expand. We thus transition into the "longest" time, while observing the details of the melody that is slowing down, as if we were watching the details of a microcosm. (Here I will allow myself a comparison with looking through a microscope). And even though we try to accelerate the melody and restore to it its previous track, we are not successful in accomplishing that. This is good. The melody is for good removed from its initial track and located, for good, "at home" on another axis, another, greater track of a greater time. We do not feel a need to return, but we decelerate with pleasure. And we have not fallen into an abyss? ...Quite the contrary. For over 10 minutes we follow the track of the music of "long" times, while closely observing its details, without thinking about anything, only perceiving, only feeling... Feeling what?

"Hypnotized," we await for what is inevitable...

I should add that in this concerto I alternate the following:

Instrumentation that is *focused* — e.g., small divisi strings, or its absence, concrete doublings in the prime and octave of set harmonic vertical complexes in wind instruments, doubling at the prime in the strings (playing on two strings a prime in the greatest possible span), etc. — this gives me the possibility of a better capturing of the flow of musical action, a possibility of a better acceleration of this action, that is of oscillation in "short" times. The focused instrumentation helps also to accomplish a more clearly legible heterophony.

The *expansive* instrumentation — that is large, or very large divisi mostly in the strings, spectral harmonies, wide harmonic arrangements of vertical chords, etc. — that gives me a possibility to better penetrate the details of musical action, its harmony, a possibility of a better deceleration of this action, that is (as it were) "dissembled" into its prime factors, and therefore, better oscillating in the "long" times. (Here, we look at harmony through the microscope....)

≈ In Summary ≈

I could still talk and dissemble into prime factors my "compositional kitchen." I could describe the music, measure by measure, phrase after phrase, but what for? Ultimately, it cannot be named by words... If it were possible... ah, I would have been writing books.

What could have been described and was, I defined as effectively as I could, while focusing mainly on my musical and not only musical philosophy. Therefore, as I had earlier mentioned — the whole aesthetics of my music stems from my philosophy. Never *vice versa*. And my philosophy stems from my perceptions and experiences. My philosophy is my music.

~ Hanna Kulenty

≈ BETWEEN KITSCH AND SURREALISM ≈

Hanna Kulenty

Lecture at an event of Helena Modjeska Art & Culture Club in Los Angeles, South Pasadena, California, September 2017

Ladies and Gentlemen,

To look at the tension, the path or the connection between kitsch and surrealism, it is necessary to approximate, illuminate these phenomena first and then look for a possible connection between them, if that connection even exists.

In my opinion there is no link between kitsch and surrealism. Just as there is no connection between kitsch and art. We have a work of art, or we have kitsch and that is it! But the tension between these phenomena exists. Of course, it exists, or otherwise I would not touch the subject. The tension exists in the so-called "Interpretation of Art." This tension exists in the "interpretation of surrealism" itself.

So the tension exists in practice, because — unfortunately — it often happens that something that is written by the composer and considered a work of art, turns out to be kitsch. The tension exists because kitsch exists, and it would be better if kitsch did not exist, or at least if there was as little of it as possible...

Fortunately, we often deal with the opposite case. Something that is supposed to be kitsch, something said to resemble kitsch, turns out to be a real work of art. This is where a higher school of artistic inspiration is revealed: — how to consciously manipulate kitsch so that it becomes a work of art. Isn't it just something! Two minuses give a plus... etc.

In spite of everything, I think that too much kitsch hangs around the concert halls and not just the concert halls, one might say — there is also too much kitsch in life...

I deliberately used the terms "interpretation of art," and in a moment I corrected it to the "interpretation of surrealism," because for me, it is actually the same, it is equivalent. The word "surrealism" is, in my logical conviction, the equivalent of the word "art" — the equivalent of the term "art." I may explain this in the following way:

What is art? As the name implies in various languages of the world, art stems from "artificial", art — "artificial", Kunst - "kunstmatig," etc. Art is a worthy, noble, honest imitation of nature. It is the noble and exalted interpretation of nature - as one may prefer to call it.

Imitating the glissando of a flying airplane, or imitating a whirring glissando of the wind, rattling in the tree crowns (can you hear it?). The interpretation of the singing of birds, dolphins, whales, bees, frogs, cicadas, even humans, in all their perfection... — this for me is art.

Art is perfection! Art is an attempt to touch metaphysics, an attempt to subdue the phenomenon of time, an attempt to purify the so-called. soul — through katharsis, and the body — through emotion.

I have recently watched falling stars. They flew to the northwest, every few minutes, much faster than the evading planes, which together with these stars formed a mystical counterpoint: earthly planes, here and now, and extraterrestrial stars, billions of years old, whose light is reaching me ...

Mystical nature. Cosmos. Every thing (so to say) in its own time ... And I pick these different times, I look and embrace them with my consciousness. subconsciousness, super-consciousness, I would like to say surreal consciousness...

I'm moved by it. I'm thrilled by the size of the universe and my own smallness...

Someone once made a movie. I watched it on Facebook: the camera watched the falling stars for 24 hours and then the tape was sped up to last for less than a minute. Well... this makes an impression.

Is this art? The noble imitation of nature? An honest interpretation of nature? I guess so... (I wonder though). Are we sure?

For me, I think so, but I'm not entirely convinced. Something is missing for me there... Maybe more mystical spider webs, combining real time with unreal time?

I will say yes: it was a good idea, but the performance? — Not necessarily so... But these falling stars impressed me anyway (so to say) "in the original" thus something lit up in my soul and my brain, I got inspired...

What is art? Another conclusion comes to mind: art is the acceleration or the deceleration of the natural time. It is to make the time of nature un-real, it is to make nature un-real, it is to make time itself unreal. And so, we may enumerate further:

Art is goodness, beauty and wisdom at the same time.

This action is sometimes straightforward, and often not straightforward, and "diagonally" through our consciousness, subconsciousness or super-consciousness. Let us understand this "in the undertext", the mind "in the under-text" — so you should feel, assimilate and draw conclusions as noble as noble as art is noble, or, at least, as noble as art should be.

The arts ennoble us — it is a famous saying, I did not invent it... Art should ennoble us. I expect this from art. I think you expect it too.

Art is pure and independent, or at least it should be. One could still list, discover and enjoy more and more definitions of art, to clarify its meaning.

But what is surrealism?

A direction in art. We know that already. Everything that is detached from reality is unreal.

I am a composer who consciously joins the musical elements in such a way as to change them and especially change their times... I try to stretch a melody, for instance, so that the apparent lack of contact with this melody would tickle our senses in the subconscious. Or I'm trying to accelerate that melody so that the fluid glissandi it would enter into our superconsciousness, leaving us dissatisfied when we try to guess its prosody, its structure... (So this is such a little bit literary name of my technique, my surrealism...).

Surrealism, for me, is also equivalent to art — as I said before, because art is also detached from reality. Because art is also sur-real. Isn't it? Sur... What does it mean? More than? Above ? Under? Northwest of our consciousness, or southeast of our dreams?

No matter from which side we look at it, the spiral is still going to meet somewhere, and the symmetry of the universe will continue to breathe as it has been breathing until now. (at least I hope so...)

So, if art is a respectable, dignified interpretation of the "breath" of the universe, it is noble, because it is a sur-real imitation of nature by accelerating or slowing down its times... — thus, we can say that surrealism is the same. Also as an direction in art.

Yes, sur-real is noble!... Interesting... True? Sur-real, detached from reality is noble... For me, yes. Why? At the end, I do not know why... I said so, but that's how I feel!

This is Something we do not know until the end, but we want to know, not too fast, not too slow... In its own time. Not necessarily terrestrial time...

What, therefore, is kitsch?

When and where is the border between kitsch and art located? Between kitsch and surrealism?

And why is this border different for each person? It is somewhat different, because we are different from each other. But, well, "but"... Kitsch sooner or later is kitsch and that is. Isn't it?

Why are we filled with disgust when listening to certain musical pieces? Why are we ashamed of our neighbor (to say so) and we are upset that something like this is happening at all?

Because kitsch is a phenomenon, let me name it in general — that is not noble, not honest, not good.

Kits does not ennoble, on the contrary, kitsch upsets and annoys. Kitsch does not imitate or interpret noble nature.

There is no sublime "under," "over," "sur"... but a coarse "for" from "too much," and "no," to "not this way."

Kitsch imitates nature in a simplified, coarse way. Just: simplistic, not simple... There is a difference between coarse simplification and simplicity...

Imitating someone's imitation of nature, or imitation of someone's art, is kitsch.

How can one copy someone's perfection, someone's attempt to "subdue", someone's attempt to sur-realize or "un-realize" nature? Is it not better to "bet" (if I may say so) on yourself and count on your own imagination, hearing and talent?

Kitsch does not "give away" to nature its longer or shorter periods of time... but, instead, it shamelessly juggles too many... "secondary dominans"... (with all due respect to the dominants).

Kitsch does not understand and does not feel the "breath" of the universe.

Kitsch imitates someone's art, kitsch imitates surrealism... Imitates without understanding and without feeling.

Ladies and Gentlemen, let me quote my favorite writer Olga Tokarczuk, with whom I completely agree. Thus:

"Kitsch is an empty, unreflective imitation of what has been truly experienced, what was discovered for the first and only time. Kitsch is secondary, it is duplication, mimicry, something that tries to use once created form. Kitsch imitates emotion, burying its elemental, original affection and dressing it in content that is too tight. Kitsch, it's a force for emotion. Anything that pretends to be the same, is kitsch. Every imitation is morally wrong. That's why kitsch is dangerous. Nothing is as dangerous to man as kitsch! Even death ... "

So... Why is kitsch so dangerous? More dangerous than death?... And what is death?

If we assume that life is a "small dream" and death is a "big dream," then in fact, kitsch is dangerous, because we will wake up from every dream. We will wake up from the little dreams, as we do every day, and we will wake up from the big ones — this idea appears in all religions of the world. This is the so-called faith. I believe in "small" dreams and in "big" dreams. I watch them every day and night. And I create, the more fiercely, the more tightly, as the "big dream" drills in my subconsciousness, reminding myself of its existence.

Why are we talking about this now? Is it because to say that at first glance "big" dreams and "little" dreams are kitsch? Kitschy, because a person is the likeness of another person? Is the person in itself a kitsch? After imitating another person since birth?

Well... How to avoid human kitsch if such a thing exists?

A human being is a part of nature, and if nature works well, if it, in a noble and humble way cooperates, a human being will find agreement with nature and without too much exaggeration, Then there is no problem.

If something is yours, created from your experience and endowed with your sensibility, then neither you, nor your creation can ever be called kitsch. It is authentic. Real.

At a glance, you do not have to be kitsch neither when you mimic nature in a dignified way, nor when nature is too fussy, and you imitate it too literally...

You are kitsch when you forcefully beautify these "small" and "big" dreams... When you do not allow them to flow simply, as they are, by humbly adapting your artistic capacity to a noble imitation of nature. When, instead, you "lick your fork" that you stuck in the "plate of the proportions of the universe".

You rounded the vagueness of life and death so much that became pseudo-purity and pseudo-intelligibility. Everything must be pure and understandable. Study it, study that... Science this, science that... You drank three percent of your brain's volume, and you think you're the navel of the world.

And I'm asking why? Why? Why, for example, can you not acknowledge that there are ghosts, even though you have not seen them?

One sees the other does not see... You tell me: science is that, science that... And thus, you are "trampling around, chasing your own tail."

Ladies and Gentlemen, Of course, everything has the right to exist, even kitsch. From a logical standpoint, let there be kitsch. There must be a contrast between good and evil to distinguish at all... — philosophical point of view...

There is kitsch, surrealism, art. We have a democracy. But does democracy exist in art?

There is no democracy in art! There should be democracy in art. That's my opinion.

I deny myself saying that everything has the right to be. But I do not want kitsch, neither in art nor in the nature of the unreflective and without people. I do not want hypocrites!

I want as many artists as possible, and in the way of life and in art.

It is better to be an artist than a hypocrite. And the difference between the artist and the hypocrite is that the artist shows his own emotions and that the hypocrite is someone else.

Here is my private, minor digression:

Either someone is an artist or not. I do not believe in such a concept "the artist is going on"... But how "happens" and when? Glimmer of intuition? Glimmer of genius? One-time inspiration? Good and that... But I think that either someone has something to say in art or not! And there is no tragedy here. For everyone there is a place to be found in our terrestrial realm... No...? What is kitsch? Kitsch is hypocritical.

To end today's lecture, I would like to take a look again on the issue of any connections between surrealism and kitsch, between art and kitsch.

And where is the tension, omitting my gnashing teeth at the sight of hypocrites?

Well, I believe that there is no connection between kitsch and art, or as you like - between kitsch and surrealism. I do not see it, I do not find it! Either art, or kitsch and that's it!

Of course, the tension between these phenomena exists. It certainly exists. This tension is because there is kitsch, and it would be good if kitsch did not exist at all, or at least, it would be as limited as possible... And to have the least amount of hypocrisy, and it would be best to have no hypocrisy at all.

Hypocrisy hurts. I do not like hypocrites! I just do not like hypocrites and the effects of their actions. I do not like it anymore! This is unfortunately a common practice. In reality, there are a lot of hypocrites and a lot of kitsch. Too many, too much...

Here I will quote myself: *"Not every set of words is poetry, and not every set of sounds is music."*

It would be good if every composer was a creator... The amount of kitsch would be reduced...

Well... what to do? How to live with this kitsch?

You have to learn to live by doing what is yours!

So, let's do our thing! Let us interpret nature through your own emotions, not others.

What i+f something can sometimes be similar to something else? If it is yours, then rate yourself — your sensitivity when you commit plagiarism, or when you throw in too many secondary dominants, and when you do not do enough.

Of course, under the key-word of "interpretation" imitation threads can be hidden, but it is you, yourself, who have to feel the right balance and you as the Artist who has to feel the balance.

Hypocrites, under the key term "interpretation," will usurp the right to shameless imitation of one's feelings, emotions, or creative inspirations. A hypocrite would avoid responsibility for attempting to imprison himself in someone else's emotions, for instance, in the thrust of someone else's suspended dominant...

Interpretation, even imitation — yes. But provided that you own, sincerely and honestly what you create. That you have digested it through your own talent (generally speaking).

Only your own creative behaviors will bring imitation of nature, the noble and honest kind. Its own creative element imitates every imitation, giving it a new value. An unique value - because it is yours, because you are unique! It is a different value, even though it may be similar to someone else's value. But it is yours! Do not be afraid of this man, composer, artist!

And so, you will sooner or later, be similar more or less to someone like you, but, still, you will be different! We are not clones, and even if, we were clones of each other, the combinations and permutations of orchestral instruments are not yet exhausted... There is enough for the future generations...

Be human yourself and do not undermine nature. Do not deal with idle "inventing"...

Dig into your own under... reality, over... reality, under... consciousness, over... consciousness...

Sur... Sur... Consciousness...

Be a human being, a composer, a beautiful artist, that is beautifully different, both in art, and in life! There is enough space for everyone...

Let us all be beautifully surrealist...

~ Hanna Kulenty

≋ DIMENSIONS OF TIME & EMOTION ≋
≋ THE MUSIC OF HANNA KULENTY ≋

By Maja Trochimczyk

Expanded version of an essay "Kulenty and the Sonic Geometry of the Heart" published in Hana Kulenty's Composer's Brochure by Donemus, 2003

The emotional intensity, structural clarity, temporal coherence and sheer sonorous impact of the music of Hanna Kulenty add up to create an original and fascinating sound world that could be summed up in the phrase: "the sonic geometry of the heart." The composer seeks a full personal involvement of her listeners, an engagement of their feelings and thoughts. Her music — whether worked out with detailed architectural designs or sketched in a spontaneous outpouring of creativity — resonates with the richness of her internal life. While listening to the vast sonorous arches, slowly rising to powerful climaxes in her Violin Concerto No.2 (1996), or in *A Fourth Circle* for violin and piano (1994), one inevitably recalls Rainer Maria Rilke's poetic description of music as "feelings transformed into audible landscape."

Sound as volume; sound as breath, as motion, as change itself: sound as life. Hanna Kulenty's music is permeated with images of organic transformation and growth, from *Breathe* for string orchestra (1987), through *Perpetuus* (1989), and *Air* (1991) for chamber ensemble. The intuitive shaping of evolving sound patterns, extended phrases and richly detailed textures in these works results from Kulenty's original compositional technique which she calls "the polyphony of arches" or "arcs." The works include many layers of simultaneous "arches" which may begin at different points of their trajectories and proceed at different speeds. From *Sesto* for solo piano (1986) to *Trigon* (1989) for ensemble, Kulenty juxtaposed several textural layers of growing intensity (rising tempi, register, dynamics) in complex patterns of ebb and flow. In *Trigon,* for instance, during a climax the third arch enters at the height of its intensity, branching out from the previous one. Yet, even in the most geometrically-titled pieces (such as *Arcus* for percussion, 1986; or the series of *Circles,* from Third to Sixth, for various solo instruments and piano and/ or electronics, 1994-1996) the images are never concrete evocations or representations of objects, rather, they evoke shifting emotional states of a great intensity and scope.

Composing with thick layers of simultaneous 'arcs' often calls for vast instrumental resources; hence the oeuvre of Kulenty includes three symphonies and many concerti for soloists accompanied by the symphony orchestra: three for piano (1990, 1992, 2003), two for violin (1993, 1996), three for flute (written between 2001 and 2018), three for trumpet (written between 2002 and 2014), one each for saxophone (2015), viola (2015), and harpsichord (2009), and one for two cellos (2018). Some concerti bear different titles, for instance *Ad Umbro* (2020) for pan flute and symphony orchestra, *Alinea* for clarinet, piano and orchestra (2021), or *Aisthetikos* (2022) for soprano saxophone, piano and orchestra. But there even is a *Concerto Rosso* for string quartet and string orchestra! (2017).

Kulenty's preferred medium has been the symphony orchestra which has the richest sound palette, though recently she has written numerous chamber-music works. Her compositional style has evolved during the years since her dazzling orchestral debut, *Ad Unum*, written in 1985 for her graduation from the Chopin Academy of Music in Warsaw, Poland. *Ad Unum* is a powerful, dissonant, dramatic and well-crafted study of convergence towards musical unity; with a large-scale architectural plan realized through massive, mobile sonorities. Favoring the sonic richness of the symphony orchestra, she explored its full range of sonorities and volumes in three Symphonies (No. 1 of 1986, No. 2 of 1987, and No. 3 of 1998-99), numerous other works for symphony orchestra, from *Trigon* of 1989 to *InfiniInfini* of 2004, and a dozen or so of concerti.

Her orchestral style has initially been compared to that of Penderecki, Xenakis, or Ligeti; she has shared their flair for drama, expressive intensity, layering of thick and fluctuating textures, as well as a relentless motion of continuously evolving sonorities. The turn towards a unique version of minimalism in the 1990s works may be attributed to studying with Louis Andriessen, most of whose students write "minimalist-oriented" pieces. Kulenty calls this phase in her works "European trance music" and often structures her compositions as single, powerful arcs. However, the emergence of her original style of "trance music" may have been impacted less by Andriessen than by her student experience at the summer courses for composers in Darmstadt, Germany. One year, she participated (as a page-turner) in an entrancing, multi-hour performance of Morton Feldman's Second String Quartet. Having experienced the hypnotic effect of extreme slowing-down of musical flow, she did not imitate Feldman, but rather developed a unique philosophy of trance perception and musical time.

Good examples of this style are provided by *A Fourth Circle* for violin and piano (1994) and *A Sixth Circle* for trumpet and piano (1995). The melodic instrument in *A Fourth Circle* could be a violin, viola or cello; the work is most frequently performed in the violin version. It was premiered at the New Music Festival, Musikhost, in Odense, Denmark, in 1994; the main theme of the festival was 'Three Polish

Women: Bacewicz, Moszumańska-Nazar, and Kulenty.' *A Sixth Circle* for trumpet and piano, premiered in 1998 in Los Angeles, shares the melodic traits with its predecessor: microtonal inflections and long stretches of held notes in the trumpet, as well as driving ostinati in the piano. Kulenty credits her intuition and the subconscious as the sources for the haunting sonorities and compelling emotional intensity of the music she creates.

Her sound world is unmistakably her own: even fragments of large-scale works, such as *Sinequan Forte A* for cello and orchestra (1994), or *Certus* (1997) for orchestra, bear the mark of her musical personality, the imprint of her harmonic language and her rhythmic drive. The remarkable consistency of form, as the composer explains, results from her method of composing: she first hears or "envisions" (in sounds and time) the whole work in its entirety, in a point that contains all of its dimensions, and later writes down this momentary musical vision by "stretching out" or extending in time layers of musical material that appeared in a condensed form in the initial "revelation" of the given piece. Interestingly, the aesthetic world of her orchestral works, both with solo instruments and without soloists, leans toward the late-20th century symphonic ideal: large-scale developments, sharply-chiseled contours of sonorous masses, and a profound seriousness of expression. The word "sublime" comes to mind as the best label for what in Kulenty's style is recognizably, grandly, romantic. The similarity, though, ends at the level of expression, and does not extend to details of musical language. Kulenty never quotes other composers' music, not even when referring to their style. In need, she would rather write her own fugue in the style of Bach than cite one of his.

Nonetheless, Kulenty's music is far from being expressively monolithic: its emotional trajectory leads from dramatic intensity to elusive moments of tranquility, especially in the cadenzas of works with solo instruments, or before the concluding segments of her compositions. Kulenty's delicate, multihued sound fabrics arise from a polyphony of graceful sonorous strands (extended, slow glissandi) surrounded by shimmering sound planes (created by trills, tremolo, flutter tongue effects and frequently appearing microtonal harmonies). These subtle, constantly shifting musical layers bear a curious resemblance to patterns of undulating lines in the abstract designs of Kulenty's graphic art (drawing and paintings, even some wall designs and tile patterns in her home!). This deep-level similarity indicates that these recurring gestures stem from a level of creative personality placed beyond the purely musical.

The remarkable consistency of her musical personality and a constant quest for new forms of expression of her inner sound world do not entail rejecting the traditional sonorities, especially the orchestra. During a seminar for Dutch composers in 2002 she explained her penchant for symphonic music in the following words:

> "People sometimes say that the symphony orchestra is finished and new sounds, new instruments should be invented to replace it. I do not agree. I think that the orchestra provides us with endless possibilities for composing music. I would compare it with the alphabet: there are only 26 letters, but poets and writers continue to create wonderful things in many languages: Polish, English, Dutch... Nobody complains that they do not have enough letters to express what they want. Similarly, the combinations of various orchestral instruments are known, they have been tried out and experimented with. Yet, each person will arrange these 'musical building blocks' in a different way. I do not even mean here the full variety of combinations and permutations of these elements.

What I mean is their arrangement in time. Each piece will have a different form, each will reflect the individual personality of the composer. It will, of course, only if the composers dare to be themselves. You have to trust and follow your intuition."

One of Kulenty's preferred dramatic gestures is the use of reflections or "doubles" of solo instruments, either by employing a second, "mirroring" instrument in the orchestra (as in her piano concerti) or by adding electronic delay to the array of performing forces (in Violin Concerto No.1, *Cadenza* of 1992; *Sinequan* of 1993 and its orchestral counterparts; *A Fifth Circle* for flute, *A Sixth Circle* for trumpet and piano) These sonorous mirrors create an air of nostalgia in the music that sounds as if it were "remembered" or "reflected upon" already in its unfolding. Achieving the emotional impact that Kulenty requires presents a great challenge for performers.

Formidable technical difficulties make *One by One* (1988) for solo marimba and *Arci* for solo percussionist (1986) showpieces of instrumental virtuosity. The challenge in solo compositions for melodic instruments *(Still Life with a Violin* of 1985, *Still Life with a Cello* of 1993; *A Fifth Circle* for alto flute of 1994, or *La Scala Solo* for trumpet of 2020) lies in musical and expressive difficulties, i.e. sustaining the continuity of a melodic line through silences and creating a sense of continuing motion throughout the span of the work. This "rhapsodic playfulness" with musical time remains another hallmark of Kulenty's oeuvre. Her *Harmonium* (1999) expanded the image of the harmonium as an oversized accordion, with its strangely shifting "oom-pah" accompaniment figures and continuous, sinuous line of melodic figuration. The effect of shifting harmonies and "breathing" dynamics is strangely disconcerting as if the instrument had a life of its own and took the unwitting performer on a drunken adventure through harmonic mists and mistakes. Here Kulenty's focus on musical time revealed its humorous dimension.

Kulenty's works for chamber groups and soloists are notably less somber than those for symphony orchestra or the stage. Here the listener may find delightful reflections of jazz patterns (*Going Up* for ensemble, 1995; *MM-Blues* for two pianos and two percussionists, 1999; or *TapBlowDance* of 2020). Then, there are humorous pastiches of musical conventions (*Stretto* for flute, clarinet and guitar, 1998). Music for non-traditional ensembles may bring together a gamelan with pre-recorded tape (*Lysanxia*, 1994), or an accordion, string orchestra and percussion (*E-motion*, written for her doctorate in 2011).

In general, her writing for solo instruments remains well attuned to the instruments' characteristics and performance techniques; a pianist by training, Kulenty is equally at home writing for the strings, percussion and winds. Her particular favorites were: the violin, with pieces penned for Krzysztof Bakowski; cello — for Andrzej Bauer; trumpet — for Marco Blaauw; flute — for Jadwiga Kotnowska; and saxophone — for Alina Mleczko. Many works were commissioned and given their premiere by the Dutch ensemble, De Ereprijs, conducted and produced by Wim Boerman. With this group as Kulenty's most faithful supporter, the number of her aficionados among Dutch performers steadily grew.

Through the 1990s, the composer developed an original version of "post-minimalist" style, characterized by a reduction of the number and density of musical layers, in comparison with the earlier, saturated and dramatic style of the "polyphony of arches." She called this style her version of the "European trance music" (though she pointed out its parallels in extended time scales and meditative qualities of Indian ragas, rather than Western minimalism). Her shift in this direction was partly affected by her post-graduate studies with Louis Andriessen, who for every new piece reduces his material in such a way as to create a specific compositional and philosophical problem.

Unlike most of Andriessen's students, however, Kulenty seldom used sudden textural cuts and shifts in this period. Instead, she often structured her compositions as single, powerful arches, slowly evolving in time, gradually increasing their gripping intensity of emotion. Good examples of this style are provided by her cycle of works titled after successive "circles" though not written in that order (*A Fourth Circle* for violin and piano and *A Fifth Circle* for alto flute with electronics, both of 1994; *A Sixth Circle* for trumpet and piano, 1995; and *A Third Circle* for piano solo, 1996). The pervasive repetitiousness of evolving melodic phrases and the insistence of fast-pulsed, obsessively rhythmic patterns in these works suggest their kinship to post-minimalism. Simultaneously, though, it brings to mind the Baroque technique of" spinning-out" used in preludes and toccatas of Johann Sebastian Bach; other associations include, surprisingly in this context, the dissonant and intense music of Iannis Xenakis. Kulenty's large-scale formal designs, built with her own, characteristic sonorities, harmonies, and phrases (her "imprint" on her music is as unmistakable as Xenakis' or Andriessen's on theirs), endow even the smallest chamber compositions with a monumental, symphonic quality.

Kulenty's penchant for musical drama and intensity of emotion found a suitable expression in her music for stage. The "intuitive constructivism" coupled with a heightened emotional intensity of her music is well-suited for highlighting dramatic situations. These traits are apparent already in her early monodrama to texts from *Three Women* by Sylvia Plath, entitled *The Parable of the Grain* (1985). Her chamber opera, written in 1996 on commission from the

Munich Biennale and given its premiere by the Hamburg Opera, *The Mother of Black-Winged Dreams*, explores the difficult subject matter of the "multiple personality syndrome" and touches upon issues of intense personal suffering, including schizophrenia and the dark themes of child abuse. Due to the seriousness of the subject matter and its unique presentation, soon after its creation the opera was discussed in a doctoral dissertation by philosopher Stefan Feltes (1999). With the scenario penned by a Canadian writer, poet and sound artist, Paul Goodman (active in the Netherlands for the past 20 years), the opera is structured as one huge arch of increasing tension, spanning the duration of the piece. Multiple voices, whisper and laughter rise and fade on the tape; multiple personalities shift and change on the stage... In January 1997, American music critic, Alan Rich, praised Kulenty's opera for its "clean, bright minimalist style that seems simple and then gets under your skin" and gives the listener "the feeling of floating in time and space." Kulenty's mastery of time and her ability to structure her musical material into layers moving inexorably, inevitably towards powerful climaxes brings a symphonic dimension to her other theatrical compositions, including the ballet *Elfen* (1997), written for the Duch chamber orchestra, De Ereprijs.

The second opera, *Hoffmanniana*, completed in 2003, brings together Kulenty's fascination with time expressed in her technique of the "polyphony of time dimensions" and her interest in stark existential subjects. The opera's libretto by Dutch writer and stage director Erick Aufderheyde is based on an unrealized film scenario by Andrei Tarkovsky, enriched with fragments from Tarkovsky's personal diary dating from 1986, the year he died. The libretto's basic idea is to mirror the lives of Tarkovsky and Hoffmann: the opera begins from Tarkovsky's last words and traces his last year backwards while simultaneously presenting the final seven days in the life of E.T.A. Hoffmann in chronological order. As a result, two contrasting time dimensions are created, allowing to present the indominable spirits of both main characters while contrasting their physical conditions. In Day Five (the beginning of the second act of the opera) they arrive at a comparable state of suffering, reaching it from opposite directions. The original film scenario is an elaborate and extended collage of episodes and people from E.T.A. Hoffmann's life and work. Yet, in *Hoffmanniana*, Tarkovsky expressed his most personal ideas about art, memory, inspiration, and creativity. Even aspects of his private life are woven into its plot.

The theme of the "double," of the man who looks in the mirror to discover a different face, or no face at all, can be traced to other films by Andrei Tarkovsky, and, interestingly, also to other musical works by Hanna Kulenty. The composer's approach to the perennial rivalry between verbal and musical layers in the opera is to transform them into simultaneous layers, with the spoken and sung texts appearing alternatively in the foreground and the background. Thus, the main characters are played by both actors and singers, who reveal different aspects of their personalities, relationships, and emotional states.

The overall formal plan follows the schema of the seven days, with four days appearing in Act One and the remaining three in Act Two. The singers present extended "arias" of cantabile and meditative material, also combining voices in duets, where the main character is accompanied by an echo, mirror, or shadows of another voice. Three large-scale climaxes of increasing intensity and duration articulated the form in Act One. The second act allows for "reverberations" of material from musically intense and complex Act One to be contemplated and organized in the listeners' memories while following a purely theatrical monologue of Hoffmann accompanied by a variety of recorded sounds: wind, children's laughter, shrill sounds of the swallows... Music gradually enters this austere sound world and the second part of Act Two is one extended dramatic and musical "crescendo" leading to the most powerful climax at the end.

The compositional technique of the "polyphony of time dimensions" emphasizes the circularity of time and the simultaneity of time-events occurring on different temporal planes. This technique emerges in *Hoffmanniana* where it supplanted the "polyphony of arches" used until about 1993-4, and the "European trance music" used until 2001. The "polyphony of time dimensions" transforms selected elements from earlier compositional techniques into a new style, making its appearance also in the Piano Concerto No. 3 (2003) and the Trumpet Concerto completed in 2002 and first performed in 2003 by Marco Blaauw as the soloist with the WOSPR Orchestra (National Polish Radio Orchestra of Katowice), under the direction of Belgian conductor Ronald Zollman. The live recording from the premiere of the Trumpet Concerto received first prize at the UNESCO Rostrum of Composers for the year 2003. With harmonic and sonorous gestures endowing the music with an unmistakable Kulenty-imprint, the Concerto reveals a composer who has mastered her resources and is able to draw from her vocabulary to highlight the virtuosity of the soloist and the rich sonorous palette of the orchestra. In the Trumpet Concerto, Kulenty shares with her listeners and performers the exhilarating joy of making music, taking them on a wild musical ride through a kaleidoscope of soundscapes, a magical *perpetuum mobile* inspired by the dance music from the Balkans.

The next stage of Kulenty's compositional technique was the "polyphony of time dimensions" that emphasizes the circularity of time and the simultaneity of time-events occurring on different temporal planes. This technique is described in her habilitation essay on her compositional philosophy of 2015, reprinted in the present volume.

Kulenty's music frequently employs sudden shifts and transitions of musical material, for instance from motoric repetitions of patterns in a quick tempo, to a slow, melancholy melody, that may be interrupted by another layer of distinct musical material. She consciously creates these sudden twists and changes in the musical narration as if to unsettle and bewilder her listeners. Thus, she creates emotional response to her music by playing with the listeners' expectations. The iteration of her technique based on setting up expectations and disappointments is known as *Musique surréalistique.*

Kulenty named this compositional technique using this French term after 2015 — even giving this title to one of her chamber music pieces of 2018 (see the essay reprinted in the present volume). In a 2020 interview with Thea Derks, the composer thus described this new technique:

> "For me it is always about emotion, in that sense every new piece is a regrouping of emotions. A collage if you like. I feel intuitively what I want to say but nowadays intuition plays a less important role when composing. I'm still averse to preconceived compositional techniques, but I no longer mind rubbing up against conventions. I make use of traditional elements, but use them as I see fit. [...] Of course the musical form is partly determined by musical parameters like proportion, balance and the like, but musique surréalistique goes further than that. It is a way of juxtaposing sound and time structures in such a way that the whole work gets a new atmosphere."

The composer then made a comparison of listening to a musical work to reading a book:

> "While reading you develop an expectation pattern. You think you know what is going to come, but are suddenly confronted with a twist that places the whole thing in a different perspective. The expected emotion can take a different form each time: it can stop, turn around, transform or remain the same. That constant tension brings you into a trance."

While discussing a specific example, Kulenty gave another explanation of what she means by *musique surréalistique*:

> "Because of the structured build-up, you expect this motoric rhythm to continue. But then suddenly a sad melody sounds and two musical worlds collide. From that moment on, a delay sets in. The music even seems to come to a standstill, but that doesn't happen, it 'freezes,' time is stopped for a moment. The tragic motif never sounds in full, so that your expectation is partly, but never one hundred percent, honored. You simply don't know when which emotion will return and in what form. So, the piece is always different and unexpected in its emotional 'expectedness.' " (Interview with Thea Derks, 2020).

In the past decade, Kulenty's stylistic range expanded due to the particular "cross-pollination" with jazz: she started performing piano improvisations as a soloist or with her favorite jazz musician, David Lewandowski. Some of their recordings may be found on Kulenty's YouTube Channel: improvisation entitled *Orange Fields* (2019) and *Aelinea Alineae* (2021) for piano, percussion and saxophone, performed by Hanna and David, with saxophonist Alina Mleczko. Lewandowski's death on 24 February 2022 ended the fruitful collaboration and was commemorated by the composer in a solo piano piece *Étoile pour David* (2023). Incidentally, Kulenty's oeuvre features two other pieces with a related title: *Étoile infini* for string quartet, and *Étoile* for voice and piano. This is an example of her inclination to compose in cycles, using variants of the same title and the same core idea in a series of compositions for different instrumental settings. This technique was discussed by Polish music theorist, Anna Nowak in 2021.

Kulenty's original world of music continues to grow with each new composition. The composer's most remarkable achievement to date is the creation of intensely emotional, stark yet enchanting music, that, to cite Rilke again, "streams towards us ... goes right through us... it is almost like a higher air, we draw it into the lungs of the spirit." In its immanent reality of sound, and haunting emotional impact, Kulenty's musical world "breathes a different air."

~ *Maja Trochimczyk*

≈ A BIOGRAPHY OF HANNA KULENTY ≈

Hanna Kulenty (born on 18 March 1961 in Białystok, Poland) is a Polish composer of contemporary classical music. Since 1992 she lives both in Warsaw (Poland) and in Arnhem (The Netherlands).

≈ Education ≈

She began her music education as a pianist in the Grażyna Bacewicz Elementary Music School in Warsaw. In 1976-1980, she studied piano performance at the Karol Szymanowski Music High School in Warsaw. From 1980 to 1986, she studied composition with Włodzimierz Kotoński at the Chopin Academy of Music in Warsaw. From 1986-1988, she did her post-graduate work in composition with Louis Andriessen at the Royal Conservatory of Music in The Hague.

In 1983-1990, she participated in the International Courses for Young Composers organized by the Polish Section of the ISCM. There, she attended lectures by Iannis Xenakis, Witold Lutosławski, Thomas Kessler and François Bernard Mâche. She was also invited for private one-on-one sessions with Lutosławski in his home: he did not formally teach composition and only interacted in this way with the most promising composition students. She attended twice the International Summer Courses of New Music at Darmstadt (1984 and 1988).

The year 1985 was very important for Kulenty's career: her composition for symphony orchestra, *Ad Unum,* received the second prize at the European Young Composers' Competition, organized in Amsterdam by the European Cultural Foundation to celebrate the continent's unity. The theme of her work, a dissonant, dramatic and well-crafted study of convergence towards musical unity, was eminently suitable for this occasion. The same piece by the 24-year-old composer, performed at the Warsaw Autumn Festival, elicited an enthusiastic response from Jan Weber, an influential music critic who warned Kulenty's male colleagues: "Gentlemen, hear and tremble!"

In 2013, she obtained her doctorate in music composition from the Karol Lipiński Academy of Music in Wrocław, working under the supervision of Prof. dr hab. Grażyna Pstrokońska-Nawratil. In 2015 she obtained her second academic degree "habilitation" (*nota bene*, not existing in American educational system), with the composition of Trumpet Concerto No. 3 and an associated essay that is reprinted in the present volume. The degree was granted by the Karol Szymanowski Academy of Music in Katowice, under the supervision of Prof. dr hab. Eugeniusz Knapik.

In 2024, Kulenty was granted Full Professorship of the Musical Arts by the President of Poland, Andrzej Duda.

≈ Career Landmarks ≈

From 1989 to the present, Kulenty has worked as a free-lance composer, supported by numerous commissions and scholarships. Kulenty composed two operas, nearly twenty pieces for large orchestra and more than 100 other works for chamber ensembles and soloists.

In 1990, Kulenty was a guest composer at Deutscher Akademischer Austauschdienst (DAAD) in Berlin. In addition to this prestigious fellowship, awarded to senior artists in many disciplines, she also received annual scholarships from the Fonds voor de Scheppende Toonkunst in Holland. In 1999-2000, she was the composer-in-residence with Het Gelders Orkest in the Netherlands. Her first major international commission was by Sender Freise of Berlin for the Symphony No. 2 for larger orchestra and mixed choir, with text from Spinoza's *Ethics* (1987). Hanna Kulenty has received numerous commissions and scholarships from the governments of Poland and Holland, and a variety of music organizations.

She lectured at the Other Minds 10 Festival (San Francisco) and at Soundstreams Canada in 2005. In that same year, she served as a guest professor at the Conservatory of Zwolle. In 2007, she was a guest professor at the ESMuC, Music Academy in Barcelona. Kulenty served as a jury member for many international events: the ISCM World Music Days (national jury in Poland, 1992), the Munich Biennale in 1995, the International Gaudeamus Music Week 2002, the International New Chamber Opera Competition "Orpheus-Luciano Berio 2003-2004", and the International Competition of Contemporary Chamber Music in Cracow (in 2005 and 2007).

After repeatedly attending International Courses for Young Composers organized by Polish Society of Contemporary Music, in 1996 Kulenty returned to Kazimierz Dolny as a featured composer and lecturer. Over the years, she gave numerous guest lectures and composition seminars in Poland, Germany, the Netherlands, Denmark, England, and the U.S. Since 2015, she has taught composition at the Feliks Nowowiejski Music Academy in Bydgoszcz, Poland; she was invited to join the faculty by her mentor in the area of teaching, Zbigniew Bujarski. She was well prepared for this step by receiving her doctorate in composition in 2013 in Wrocław, and her habilitation degree in 2015. She recently became a full professor (spring of 2024). While teaching composition, she pays special attention to her students' compositional craft, their detailed knowledge of instruments, instrumental ranges and techniques, as well as to the overall structure and temporal flow of their compositions. Prof. Kulenty teaches between 5 and 10 composition students every year. Her students appreciate the fact that she helps them overcome writing blocks or resolve structural issues in their compositions, without imposing her personal style or aesthetics.

Her music has been featured at festivals in Poland, Denmark, England, Germany, Ireland, the Netherlands, and the U.S. Her music is available on several solo CDs and has been broadcast and recorded in many European countries. Her YouTube Channel currently features 94 recordings of her music. She was a featured composer at many festivals, including a 1998 appearance at the University of Southern California in Los Angeles, where *A Sixth Circle* for trumpet and piano received its world premiere. She returned to USC for the 2022 Paderewski Lecture-Recital, an annual event of the USC Polish Music Center, honoring the most eminent Polish composers with public lectures and performances of their music. At present, Kulenty continues to serve as composition professor in Bydgoszcz, Poland, while composing on commission from such famous institutions as the Kronos String Quartet or the London Symphony Orchestra.

≈ Compositions ≈

Hanna Kulenty writes for solo instruments, chamber groups of various sizes, and large orchestras. She composed two operas, as well as music for several television plays and feature films. Her compositions have been premiered during festivals throughout the world, including such well-known events as the Huddersfield Festival, Schleswig-Holstein Musik Festival, Münchener Biennale, Warsaw Autumn, Musica Polonica Nova and the Netherlands Music Days. Her numerous orchestral pieces have been performed by symphony orchestras in Holland, Denmark, Poland and Germany, with conductors like David Porcelijn, Antoni Wit,

Peter Hirsch, Peter Eötvös, Ingo Metzmacher, Renato Rivolta and Ronald Zollman.

Soloists that performed her music include violinist Isabelle van Keulen, harpsichordist Elżbieta Chojnacka, violinist Krzysztof Bąkowski, flutist Jadwiga Kotnowska, saxophone-player Alina Mleczko, trumpet player Marco Blaauw and pianist Frank Peters. Many works were premiered by the Dutch ensemble 'de ereprijs', that commissioned her to write music for their concerts and performances, including the ballet *Elfen*. In 2008 and 2011 she was commissioned by Kronos Quartet for whom she wrote her 4th and 5th string quartets.

She wrote four symphonies and numerous concertos for such diverse instruments as piano, harpsichord, violin, viola, cello, two cellos, flute, saxophone, and trumpet. These concerti were often commissioned by the soloists or designated for specific musicians. For instance, trumpet concerti were inspired/performed by trumpet-players Marco Blaauw and Kulenty's son, Piotr Majoor.

A noted British composer and music historian, Prof. Adrian Thomas, thus described the early evolution of Hanna Kulenty's compositional technique in an entry about her in *The Oxford Music Online* (2003): "*Kulenty established the essential parameters of her compositional practice while still a student: works such as* Ad unum *and* Sesto *contain percussive rhythm and iterative gestures, while formally they carry a sense of momentum. The clarity of her writing — which varies from unison pedal points to differently paced musical strata, as in* Trigon *(1989) — is largely the realization of a compositional strategy, the 'polyphony of arcs'. Overlapping or in sequence, these determine small-and-large-scale events, and are governed, for example, by chordal progressions, timbral effects or emotional intensity. Much of her material draws on phenomena such as inhalation-exhalation and spectral harmony."*

The next period, starting ca. 1994, brought in a change of style, accomplished by slowing down and lengthening the musical arches or layers of material that intersect and become audible or inaudible, leading to a dramatic structure of the music. The number of these "arcs" is indicated in the work's title, for instance Sesto for piano (1985) included six such musical layers, whereas in *Quatro* and *Quinto* (1986) there were four and five arcs respectively. In the mid-1990s, the number of these arcs was limited, and their velocity slowed down, for instance the opera *The Mother of Black-Winged Dreams* (1996) consisted of one extensive arc of growing dramatic intensity, evolving throughout the opera.

Kulenty's preferred medium is the symphony orchestra, but her penchant for musical drama and intensity of emotion found a suitable expression in her music for stage. In December 1996, the Hamburg Opera premiered *The Mother of Black-Winged Dreams* at the Munich Biennale. The opera explores the difficult subject matter of "multiple personality syndrome" and touches upon issues of suffering, child abuse, and gender relations. With the scenario penned by a Canadian writer who lives in Holland, Paul Goodman, the chamber work is structured as one huge arch of increasing tension, spanning the duration of the piece.

Since the success of this opera at the Münchener Biennale 1996 she is considered one of the leading figures on the Polish contemporary music scene. The renowned American music critic Alan Rich of *L.A. Weekly* attended the Munich performance and praised Kulenty as a rare talent of great originality and dramatic flair. He then reviewed Kulenty's 1998 Los Angeles concert, concluding: *"I will continue to sing her praises. What I have heard of Kulenty tells me of a headstrong experimenter with some powerful ideas about pounding on and rewarding a hearer's senses. Best of all was the new trumpet piece, setting a strong and shapely lyric line for the trumpet against a breathless perpetuum mobile from the piano. Her Second Piano Concerto is a knockout piece. Tell me about there not being any new composers."*

Kulenty's second opera, inspired by a screenplay of cult Russian filmmaker, Andrei Tarkovsky (1932-1986) and entitled *Hoffmanniana* (2002), still awaits its staging and the world premiere. Its complicated temporal structure of intersecting and reversing timelines is clearly articulated in the haunting and intense music. The opera juxtaposes seven last days of German Romantic poet-writer E.T.A. Hoffmann with those of Russian film-maker Andrei Tarkovsky, interlacing the two timelines, with one going forward and the other backwards.

According to a Polish music theorist, Anna Nowak, in addition to being fascinated with structuring time, the composer has a penchant of composing in cycles, that is, exploring a core idea, that may be melodic or structural, in a series of related works. Here we could mention only the series of four *Circles* from the period of the "trance music." While reviewing Kulenty's oeuvre, the scholar pointed out the existence of many such multiples: two pieces entitled *Still Life with...*, three entitled *Sinequan...*, two called *Going up...*, four *Brass No...*, two *Mezzo Tango...* and three works with titles beginning with *Smoky...* These titles end with different designations after the shared moniker that implies their kinship.

As an example, Nowak described in detail three different compositions based on the topos of the lullaby, *A Cradle Song:* "The composer used this title for 1) a song she wrote after her first daughter was born; 2) her Trio for violin, cello and piano; and 3) her String Quartet No. 4. An analysis of these works exposes a number of interesting material dependencies. The melody of the lullaby (1982) became the basis for the piano trio eleven years later (1993). It was the first piece Kulenty wrote after her daughter's tragic death."

"Several years later the power of expression emanating from this composition attracted the attention of the Kronos Quartet. They asked the composer to transpose the trio into an arrangement for a string quartet (2007). However, Kulenty decided to compose the work anew, using all the material from the existing composition. Despite preserving the dramatic outline of the trio, the expanded narrative of the quartet (it lasts 16 minutes, while the trio is 10 minutes long), appears to be a fresh embodiment of the musical idea that was first borne in the lullaby."

Despite her focus on the concert stage and live performances by orchestras, chamber ensembles, and soloists, Kulenty has found time to write film music (e.g. the Polish feature film *Hiszpanka* of 2015), as well as music for ballet and theater.

Since 2003, Kulenty's compositions are published by the Dutch publishing house Donemus; some of her earlier works were issued by PWM Editions in Poland.

≈ Awards ≈

In 1985, Hanna Kulenty was awarded the second prize of the European Young Composers' Competition organized in Amsterdam for **Ad Unum** for symphony orchestra (1985). In 1987 she was awarded the *Stanislaw Wyspianski Award* (2nd class). In the same year she was awarded the second prize by the Young Composers' Competition of the Polish Composers' Union for **Ride** for six percussionists (1987). She was also awarded prizes in the Composers' Competition from the Warsaw branch of the Polish Composers' Union: **Quinto** for 2 pianos (1986), first prize; **Breathe,** for string orchestra (1987), first prize; **Cannon** for violin and piano (1988), third prize; ***aaa TRE*** for viola, cello and double bass (1988), second prize in 1989.

In 2003, her **Trumpet Concerto** (2002) won the First Prize at UNESCO's 50th International Rostrum of Composers, for which she received the UNESCO Mozart Medal from the International Music Council. Her compositions Preludium, Postludium and Psalm (2007) and **String Quartet No. 3: Tell me about it** (2008), were chosen among the ten best Dutch compositions during the 'Toonzetters' contest in Amsterdam in 2007 and 2008.

In 2015, Prof. dr hab. Hanna Kulenty received the Annual Award of the Polish Composers' Union (ZKP) for her outstanding body of compositions, strong individuality and combination of musical vigor with interesting structural solutions.

≋ **Composer, Performer, Writer, Painter** ≋

In the second decade of the 21st century, Hanna Kulenty also started performing improvisation as a pianist, in a cross-over style hovering between jazz and contemporary music. Her favorite improvisation partner was original jazz percussionist David Lewandowski until his premature death in 2022.

Kulenty's creative endeavors are not limited the areas of music composition and performance. In 2017 she published a volume of creative fiction, employing her technique of colliding and intersecting timelines in a 500+-page narrative, published in Polish in California as *Odwrócony dom (The Inverted House,* Moonrise Press, 2017, second ed. 2023).

Finally, the year 2023 saw a flourishing of Kulenty's interest in painting — she created nearly 70 large acrylic paintings, with surrealist, structuralist, abstract, and musical overtones, and titles like *Muzyka Grawitacyjna Nr 4 (Gravitational Music*

No. 4). She recently held her first solo exhibition (May-June 2024, Warsaw). The cover of the present volume is based on her painting from the *Muzyka Grawitacyjna* series. Several other paintings have been reproduced in California State Poetry Society's *Poetry Letter* in 2024.

*Information from Hanna Kulenty's website
and other sources edited by Maja Trochimczyk*

≈ LIST OF WORKS ≈

From Hanna Kulenty's website: HannaKulenty.com

2024
InfiniInfini – for symphony orchestra, commissioned by the London Symphony Orchestra

2023
AtlantissForte – for soprano saxophone, piano and orchestra
AlineaDuo – for clarinet/saxophone and piano
Carrés Noirs – for piano quatre mains, two string orchestras and two percussions
Mémoire de Mémoire – for trumpet, bass trombone and string orchestra

2022
AtlantissDuo – for flute/clarinet/saxophone and piano
AtlantissSolo – for piano solo, commissioned as required piece for Paderewski Piano Competition
Étoile pour David – for piano solo, dedicated to David Lewandowski, *in memoriam*
Étoile Infini – for string quartet
Étoile – for voice and piano
La Scala Tutti – for trumpet and trombone solo and string orchestra
Cristal en Cristal – for carillon

2021
Alias – for woodwind quintet: flute, oboe, clarinet, bassoon, and French horn
Alinea – for clarinet, piano and orchestra

2020
Tap-Blow-Dance4 – for two bass clarinets, vibraphone, cello
Tap-Blow-Dance – for trumpet solo

La Scala solo – for trumpet solo
EldoradoEldorado – for voice and piano
There is nothing that can happen – for three voices, female choir
Alias Demo – for piano trio
Ad-Umbro – for pan flute and symphony orchestra
AisthetikosDuo – for soprano saxophone and piano

2019
Aisthetikos – for soprano saxophone, piano and orchestra

2018
Musique Surréalistique – for soprano, clarinet and piano
Fado – for piano trio
Flute Concerto No. 3 (2017/18) – for flute and symphony orchestra
Double Cello Concerto (2017/18) – for two celli and symphony orchestra

2017
Concerto Rosso – for string quartet and string orchestra

2016
When the morning light starts glowing – for string orchestra
Siesta – for violin, cello and trumpet
Smokey One – for piano solo
Smokey White – for piano quintet

2015
Saxophone Concerto No. 1 – for saxophone and symphony orchestra
Viola Concerto No. 1 – for viola and symphony orchestra
Hiszpanka feature film – film music

2014
VAN... – for piano quatre mains or two pianos, written for the state visit to Poland of King and Queen of the Netherlands
Trumpet Concerto No. 3 – for trumpet solo and symphony

orchestra (composed for her habilitation post-doctoral degree)
String Quartet No. 6

2013
Smokey Eyes – for double trio (two pianos, saxophone, flute, and two drumkits)
Five for Five – String Quintet No 1 (2013)
Viola-Viva – for viola and chamber orchestra
Emotionsolo – for accordion solo

2012
Cembalo Uno – for harpsichord solo

2011
E-motions – for accordion, string orchestra and percussion (composed for her doctoral degree)
String Quartet No. 5, commissioned by the Kronos Quartet

2010
Decimo Forte – for choir and ensemble
Music for Roy – for mixed choir and chamber orchestra
Twenty-five – for symphony orchestra

2009
GG Concerto – for harpsichord and string orchestra
G for G – for harpsichord solo
Sugar-Fela Tango – for piano and four instruments
Walz in A – for piano

2008
Walz from Lost & Found - twenty five – for piano and trumpet
Lost & Found - twenty five – ballet music for ensemble and tape
Brass No. 4 – for tuba solo or other brass instrument

2007
String Quartet No. 4 (A Cradle Song) commissioned by the

Kronos Quartet
Kisses & Crosses – for piano and percussion
Preludium, Postludium and Psalm – for cello and accordion
Preludium and Psalm – for harmonium or another keyboard instrument solo
String Quartet No. 3 – Tell me about it

2006
Tell me about it 2 – for bass clarinet, cello, trombone and double bass
Tell me about it 1 – for clarinet, cello, trombone and piano
Island (2006) – a stage work for trumpet solo, voice, ensemble and tape

2005
Brass No. 3 – for horn solo or trumpet solo
Brass No. 2 – for horn and trumpet
Mezzo Tango 2 – for ensemble

2004
Brass No. 1 – for trumpet solo
Run – for flute and piano
Postcard from Europe – for ensemble
Mezzo Tango – for brass band

2003
Rainbow 3 – for piano and two wind instruments
Piano Concerto No. 3 – for piano and orchestra
Hoffmanniana – opera in two acts to a libretto based on a screenplay by Andrei Tarkovsky

2002
Trumpet Concerto – for trumpet solo and symphony orchestra

2001
Crossing Lines – for violin, clarinet, and piano
Asjaawaa – for mezzo soprano, flute, harp, piano, percussion,

electronics

Flute Concerto No. 1 – for flute (amplified, delay) and chamber orchestra

2000
Drive Blues – for piano
Symphony No. 3 – for symphony orchestra
Decimo – for choir and six voices

1999
MM-blues – for two pianos and two percussions
Harmonium – for harmonium solo

1998
Rapidus – for saxophone quartet
Stretto – for flute, clarinet, cello, guitar
Part One – for orchestra

1997
Certus – for chamber orchestra
Waiting for... – for voice and piano
Elfen ballet music – for ensemble, commissioned by de ereprijs ensemble

1996
Sierra – for violin and cello
Violin Concerto No. 2 – for violin and orchestra
A Third Circle – for piano solo
Blattinus – for saxophone quartet

1995
The Mother of Black-Winged Dreams – opera in one act to a libretto by Paul Goodman
Going Up 2 – for ensemble
Going Up 1 – for violin and double bass
A Sixth Circle – for trumpet and piano

1994
Sinequan Forte B – for solo amplified cello with delay
A Fifth Circle – for alto flute with delay
A Fourth Circle – for violin (or viola/cello) and piano
Sinequan Forte A – for solo amplified cello with delay, orchestra
Lysanxia - for gamelan and tape

1993
A Cradle Song – for violin, cello, and piano
Sinequan (rev. 1993) – for solo cello with delay
Sinequan – for solo cello with optional delay
Violin Concerto No. 1 (orchestral version, 1993) – for violin and symphony orchestra
Still Life with a Cello – for solo cello

1992
Cadenza – for solo violin with delay
Passacaglia – for chamber orchestra
Violin Concerto No. 1 – for violin and ensemble
A few minutes for Ereprijs – for ensemble

1991
E for E – for solo harpsichord
Air – for ensemble
Piano Concerto No. 2 – for piano and orchestra

1990
String Quartet No. 2
Piano Concerto No. 1 – for piano and ensemble

1989
Trigon – for chamber orchestra
Perpetuus – for ensemble

1988
aaa TRE – for viola, cello, and double bass
One by One – for solo marimba
Souvenir from a Sanatorium – computer music
Cannon – for violin and piano
Arcus – for three percussionists

1987
Breathe – for string orchestra
Symphony No. 2 – for large orchestra and mixed choir
Ride (1987) – for six percussionists

1986
Quinto – for two pianos
Symphony no. 1 – for symphony orchestra
Arci – for percussion solo
Quatro – for orchestra

1985
Still Life with a Violin – for violin solo
Sesto – for piano solo
Ad unum – for symphony orchestra
Przypowieść o ziarnie [Parable about a grain] – chamber opera / monodrama

1984
String Quartet No. 1
Prośba o Słońce [Request for the Sun] – for electroacoustic tape
Three Minutes for the Double Bass – for double bass solo

≈ FILM AND TV MUSIC ≈

Based on Kulenty's listing on filmpolski.pl

2016 – *Feinweinblein*, TV Theater

2015 – *Hiszpanka*, Feature Film
Music Includes: *Twenty-Five, GG Concerto, Sinequan Forte B, E-Motions*

2009 – *Psie Głowy*, TV Theater
Music includes: *Elfen, 1st Piano Concerto, Harmonium, 1st Violin Concerto, Lost & Found Twenty Five, Breathe, CG Concerto*

2008 – *Kwatera Bożych Pomyleńców*, TV Theater
Music includes: *Lost & Found - Twenty Five; Walz in A, Trumpet Concerto*

2008 – *Nieruchomy Poruszyciel*, Feature Film
Music Includes: *A Third Circle, Flute Concerto No. 1, Still Life With A Cello, Preludium, Postludium And Psalm, Violin Concerto No. 2*, and fragments of *Hoffmanniana*

≈ AWARDS ≈

From Hanna Kulenty's website: HannaKulenty.com

2015 — Annual Award of the Polish Composers' Union (ZKP). Kulenty was recognized for her outstanding body of compositions, strong individuality and combination of musical vigor with interesting structural solutions.

2009 — Toonzetters, dutch composition contest.
String Quartet No. 3 . Nomination for one of the ten best new Dutch compositions of 2007

2008 — Toonzetters, dutch composition contest.
Preludium, Postludium and Psalm. Nomination for one of the ten best new Dutch compositions of 2007

2003 — UNESCO's 50th International Rostrum of Composers
Trumpet Concerto, First Prize

1989 — Competition of the Warsaw Branch of the Polish Composers' Union
aaa TRE, Second Prize

1988 — Competition of the Warsaw Branch of the Polish Composers' Union
Cannon, Third Prize

1987 — Competition of the Warsaw Branch of the Polish Composers' Union
Breathe, First Prize

1986 — Competition of the Warsaw Branch of the Polish Composers' Union
Quinto, First Prize

1987 — Young Composers' Competition of the Polish Composers' Union
Ride, Second Prize

1987 — Stanisław Wyspiański Award
Second Class Award for lifetime achievement

1985 — The 9th Wrocław One Actor's Theatre Festival, Wrocław, Poland.
Przypowieść o ziarnie *(Parable on grain),* Award for the best monodrama

1985 — European Young Composers' Competition, organized by the European Cultural Foundation, Amsterdam, Holland.
Ad Unum, Second Prize

≈ DISCOGRAPHY ≈

Edited by Maja Trochimczyk

≈ **Hanna Kulenty — Music 4.** DUX and Wrocław Philharmonics, 2011. DUX 0823). Portrait CD with 4 compositions: *GG - Concerto* (2009) for harpsichord and string orchestra; *Music for Roy* (2010) for mixed choir and chamber orchestra; *Breathe* (1987) for string orchestra; *Sinequan Forte B* (1994) for amplified cello and chamber orchestra

≈ **Hanna Kulenty meets milf.** The soundtrack of Łukasz Barczyk's film *Unmoved Mover*, 2008. Compiled by Hanna Kulenty, some tracks reworked by Polish nu-metal/punk-rock/hip-hop band 'milf'. It includes a specially composed electronic tape 'Fabryka-tapes' and parts of the compositions *Preludium, Postludium and Psalm, Flute Concerto No. 1, A Third Circle, Still life with a cello, Violin Concerto No. 2*

≈ **Arcs & Circles.** Porträtkonzert / Portrait Concert, 5. November 2000, Deutschlandfunk, 2001. The CD contains 6 works: *A Third Circle* for piano; *A Fourth Circle* for violin and piano; *A Fifth Circle*, for alto flute with delay; *A Sixth Circle*; *Arci* for percussion solo; *Stretto* for flute, clarinet, cello, guitar

≈ **First Violin Concerto,** Version for violin & ensemble. Performed by Krzysztof Bąkowski and 'de ereprijs', conducted by Wim Boerman, 1992. Live recording from a performance with a ballet by Tony Thatcher at the Arnhem School of Dance (Cenrte for New Dance Development, CNDO.)

≈ **Hanna Kulenty.** A long play record (LP) released in 1987 with *Sesto* for piano solo, *Ad unum* for symphony orchestra, and *Arci* for percussion solo. Los Angeles: Ars Polonica, 1987.

≈ **Grażyna Bacewicz, Hanna Kulenty, Elżbieta Sikora, Agata Zubel: Polish Heroines of Music. PWM CD**, PWM Edition, 2021.

≈ **Landscape of Memories**. CD of Hanna Kulenty, Zbigniew Bargielski, Roxanna Panufnik, Zygmunt Mycielski, Andrzej Panufnik, performed by BMF Piano Trio. CD Accord, 2013.

≈ **Aleksander Nowak, Marcin Stańczyk, Hanna Kulenty-Majoor, Krzysztof Penderecki. PWM CD.** PWM Edition, 2019.

≈ **No other end of the world will there be based on the works of Polish female composers of the 20th century**
Music CD by Trem Azul, 2023. Performed by Marek Pospieszalski, Piotr Chęcki, Tomasz Dąbrowski, Qba Janicki, Szymon Mika, Max Mucha, Tomasz Sroczynsi, Grzegorz Tarwid.

≈ ≈ ≈

2015 – present – Hanna Kulenty Channel on YouTube
https://www.youtube.com/channel/UCZezgv7zc1K-0qufQelX4aA

The channel features recordings from live performances of Kulenty's music, currently totaling 94 videos.

≈ ≈ ≈

≈ BIBLIOGRAPHY ≈

Edited by Maja Trochimczyk

Cordula, Jasper. *Zur Ästhetik der musikalishen form bei Werken für Schlagzeug solo.* Master's Thesis. Berlin: Technische Universitat, 1996. [analysis of Arci]

Derkowska, Aneta. *Operowe laboratorium: hybrydy gatunkowe w polskiej twórczości operowej drugiej połowy XX wieku.* Toruń: Marszałek Development & Press, 2024.

Derks, Thea. "Frenzied Heroine in Opera Hanna Kulenty" (Review of *The Mother of Black-Winged Dreams*), Cultuurpers website, 2016. https://cultureelpersbureau.nl/en/2016/07/insane-heroine-opera-hanna-kulenty/

Derks, Thea. "Composer Hanna Kulenty: 'I assemble emotions" on Derks's blog Contemporary Classical, September 2020, https://theaderks.wordpress.com/2020/09/25/composer-hanna-kulenty-i-assemble-emotions/

Du Plessis, Amoré, *The style transformation in Hanna Kulenty's string ensemble works composed between 1984 and 2013.* University of Pretoria Department of Music, 2012

Hausenplas, Piotr. *Zagadnienia wykonawcze triów fortepianowych Ludomira Różyckiego, Andrzeja Panufnika, Hanny Kulenty, Bernarda Chmielarza.* Warsaw: Wydawnictwo Akademii Muzycznej im. Fryderyka Chopina, 2008

Homma, Martina. "Kulenty, Hanna," entry in *Komponisten der Gegenwart*, 2000.

Kager, Reinhard. "Die wunden Seele wirre Stimmen." Opernwelt 38, no. 2 (February 1997): 8-10.

Knessl, Lothar. *Gerd Kühr „Stallerhof" in Wien, Michael Obst „Solaris" und Hanna Kulenty „The mother of black-winged dreams" in München.* In *Österreichische Musikzeitschrift*, 52, 1997/03/, 49.

Krawczyk, Agata. „Udział dynamiki w kształtowaniu czasu linearnego w utworach orkiestrowych Hanny Kulenty"
Article in Polish, *Aspekty Muzyki*, 2021

Krawczyk, Dorota. "Koncepcje czasu i ich wpływ na kształtowanie formy w polskiej muzyce współczesnej." *Muzyka* 40, no. 4 (1995): 113-117.

Hanna Kulenty. Composer Brochure/Catalogue. Cracow: Polskie Wydawnictwo Muzyczne, 1993.

Hanna Kulenty Brochure. Amsterdam: Donemus, 2003.

Hanna Kulenty, "Hanna Kulenty about Her Writing Technique." *Polish Music* 27/1-2 (1992): 22-25.

Kulenty, Hanna. *Plurality in Unity, or the Way of Organizing Large-Scale Times,* essay component of the Master's Thesis, complementing the Master's Thesis in composition, written under the supervision of Prof. Włodzimierz Kotonski, Warsaw: F. Chopin Academy of Music, January 1986.

Kulenty, Hanna. *New Aspects of Using my Technique of Temporal-Spatial Polyphony in the Composition* **E-Motions** *for Accordion, Strings and Percussion.* Doctoral dissertation, complementing Doctoral Work in Composition, written under the supervision of Prof. Grażyna Pstrokońska-Nawratil. Wrocław: Karol Lipiński Academy of Music, 2012.

Kulenty, Hanna. *My Philosophy of Music. A Personal Essay to Accompany Trumpet Concerto No. 3.* Habilitation, post-doctoral degree, Karol Szymanowski Academy of Music, written under the supervision of Prof. Eugeniusz Knapik, September 2015.

Kulenty, Hanna, *Odwrócony dom* [The Inverted House], fiction book in Polish, Los Angeles: Moonrise Press, 2017. Second edition in two volumes, 2023.

Kulenty, Hanna and Monika Pasiecznik, „Muzyka jak schizofrenia" interview, in Polish. *Ruch Muzyczny*, 2010

Kulenty, Hanna, and Tomasz Czyż, „Ja tworzę, nie komponuję" interview in Polish. *Ruch Muzyczny*. 2014.

Ługowska, Marta. "A typical woman: conversation with Hanna Kulenty." *Polish Music/Polnische Musik* 24/4 (1989): 16-23.

Musikhøst 94. Tre polske kvinder: Grazyna Bacewicz, Krystyna Moszumanska-Nazar, Hanna Kulenty, moderne klassikere: Olivier Messiaen, Igor Stravinsky, danske navne. Program of New Music Festival, 23-27 November 1994, Odense, Denmark.

Nowak, Anna. „Inter-Compositional Relationships as a Research Problem in the Works of Contemporary Composers," in *Music Analysis: Historia, Theoria, Praxis,* Vol. 6, ed. Anna Granat-Janki. Wrocław: Karol Lipiński Academy of Music, 2021, pp. 97-110.

Nowak, Anna. "Kwartety smyczkowe Hanny Kulenty. Pamięć gatunku a współczesne środki ekspresji" in *Polski Rocznik Muzykologiczn*y (March 2023): 20(1):80-94

Padding, Martin. "Hanna Kulenty." In *Program Booklet, "Confrontaties" Music Festival of Young Generation Composers,* Rotterdam, 1989.

Rasmussen, Per Erland. "'Gentlemen, hear and tremble!' Komponisten Hanna Kulenty." In *Musikhost 94, Festival for Ny Musik* [program book]. Odense: Fyns Unge Tonekunstnerselskab, 1994.

Thomas, Adrian. „Kulenty, Hanna" entry in *Oxford Music Online*, Oxford: Oxford University Press, 2001.

Thomas, Adrian, "Kulenty, Hanna (18 March 1961)," entry in *The Oxford Companion to Music*, Oxford University Press, 2011.

Trochimczyk, Maja. „Kulenty and the Sonic Geometry of the Heart" article in the composer's brochure by MuziekGroep Nederland. Amsterdam: Donemus, 2003.

Warnaby, John & Elfriede Witte. "Festival Review: Fifth Münchener Biennale–Part 2." *Musical Opinion* 119, no. 1409 (September 1997): 290.

www.ingramcontent.com/pod-product-compliance
Lightning Source LLC
Chambersburg PA
CBHW071625170426
43195CB00038B/2124